3RD EDITION

DISTRIBUTED
COMPUTING

Simply In Depth

AJIT SINGH

ACKNOWLEDGEMENT

This piece of study of **Distributed Computing** is an outcome of the encouragement, guidance, help and assistance provided to us by our colleagues, Sr. faculties, Tech-friends and our family members.

As an acknowledgement , I would like to take the opportunity to express my deep sense of gratitude to all those who played a crucial role in the successful completion of this book, especially to our sr. students; this book certainly has been benefited from discussions held with many IT professionals (Ex-students) over the years it took me to write it.

My primary goal here was to provide a sufficient introduction and details of the Distributed Computing so that the students can have an efficient knowledge about the same. Moreover, it presupposes knowledge of the principles and concepts of operating environment. On the same note, any errors and inaccuracies are my responsibility and any suggestions in this regard are warmly welcomed!

Last but not the least, I pay my sincere respect and regards to my Father Late Sri. SitaRam Singh and my Daughter who're ever obliged for bearing with me from time to time and insist me to share my knowledge across the world.
[Ajit Singh]

I would like to thank the Kindle Direct Publishing team and Amazon team for its enthusiastic online support and guidance in bringing out this book.

I hope that the reader likes this book and finds it useful in learning the concepts of Distributed Computing.

Thank You !!

Ajit Singh

PREFACE

Share the knowledge,

Strengthen the surrounding......!!!

Distributed computing and application systems have become central concept of how computers are used, from web applications to e-commerce and to content distribution. Distributed systems help programmers aggregate the resources of many networked computers to construct highly available and scalable services. This book will cover both fundamental concepts in distributed computing and discuss system designs enabling distributed applications. The objectives of this book include: In-depth understanding of core concepts of distributed computing, including study of both abstract concepts and practical techniques for building system support for distributed applications; construction of distributed system components; understanding of the current state of the art in several areas of distributed computing as well as providing learners with a solid foundation for understanding and specifying distributed services, designing and analyzing distributed algorithms for reliable and fault-tolerant implementations of distributed services.

This edition aims to provide an understanding of the principles on which the distributed computing are based; their architecture, algorithms and design; and how it meets the demands of contemporary distributed applications, demonstrates knowledge of the basic elements and concepts related to distributed computing technologies. It explains the knowledge of the core architectural aspects of distributed computing, design and implement distributed applications, knowledge of details the main underlying components of distributed computing (such as RPC, file systems), use and apply important methods in distributed computing to support scalability and fault tolerance as well as explains experience in building large-scale distributed applications. The main elements of the theory of distributed computing, in a unifying approach which emphasizes the similarities between different models, when possible, or explains inherent discrepancies, when they exist.

I begin with a set of nine chapters that together cover the building blocks for a study of distributed systems. The first two chapters provide a conceptual overview of the subject, outlining the characteristics of distributed systems and the challenges that must be addressed in their design: scalability, heterogeneity, security and failure handling being the most significant. These chapters also develop abstract models for understanding process interaction, failure and security. They are followed by other foundational chapters devoted to the study of networking, interprocess communication, remote invocation, indirect communication and operating system support.

This edition covers the main elements of the theory of distributed computing, in a unifying approach which emphasizes the similarities between different models, when possible, or explains inherent discrepancies, when they exist. The set of chapters covers the important topic of middleware, examining different approaches to supporting distributed applications including distributed objects and components, web services and alternative peer-to-peer solutions.

The study/learning of Distributed Computing is an essential part of any computer science education and of course for the B.Tech / MCA / M.Tech courses of several Universities across the world. This textbook is intended as a text for an explanatory course of Distributed Computing for Graduate and Post Graduate Students of several universities across the world.

TEXTBOOK OBJECTIVES
- To learn the principles, architectures, design, algorithms and programming models used in distributed computing.
- To examine state-of-the-art distributed computing.
- To design and implement sample distributed computing.
- Students will gain an understanding of the principles and techniques behind the design of distributed computing, such as locking, concurrency, scheduling, and communication across networks.

Before Taking This Book...
Suggested Background Knowledge
No pre-requisites are enforced. However, you are expected to enter the course with graduate-level understanding of computer systems and/or computer networking,

I hope you enjoy reading this book as much as I have enjoyed writing it.....,

Distributed Computing : Simply In Depth

3rd Edition

Ajit Singh
Faculty Member
Department of Computer Science
Patna University, IND

ISBN: 979-8406572009

CONTENTS

FUNDAMENTALS

1.1 WHAT IS A DISTRIBUTED COMPUTING SYSTEM

Over the past two decades, advancements in microelectronic technology have resulted in the availability of fast, inexpensive processors, and advancements in communication technology have resulted in the availability of cost effective and highly efficient computer networks. The net result of the advancements in these two technologies is that the price performance ratio has now changed to favor the use of inter-connected, multiple processors in place of a single, high-speed processor.

Computer architectures consisting of interconnected, multiple processors are basically of two types:

Tightly coupled systems: In these systems, there is a single system wide primary memory (address space) that is shared by all the processors [Fig. 1.1(a)]. If any processor writes, for example, the value 100 to the memory location x, any other processor subsequently reading from location x will get the value 100. Therefore, in these systems, any communication between the processors usually takes place through the shared memory.

Loosely coupled systems: In these systems, the processors do not share memory, and each processor has its own local memory [Fig. 1.1(b)]. If a processor writes the value 100 to the memory location x, this write operation will only change the contents of its local memory and will not affect the contents of the memory. In these systems, all physical communication between the processors is done by passing messages across the network that interconnects the processors.

Tightly coupled systems are referred to as parallel processing systems, and loosely coupled systems are referred to as distributed computing systems, or simply distributed systems.

In contrast to the tightly coupled systems, the processor of distributed computing systems can be located far from each other to cover a wider geographical area. Furthermore, in tightly coupled systems, the number of processors that can be usefully deployed is usually small and limited by the bandwidth of the shared memory. This is not the case with distributed computing systems that are more freely expandable and can have an almost unlimited number of processors.

In short, a distributed computing system is basically a collection of processors interconnected by a communication network in which each processor has its own local memory and other peripherals, and the communication between any

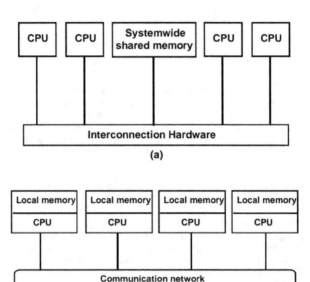

Fig. 1.1 Difference between tightly coupled and loosely coupled multiprocessor systems (a) a tightly coupled multiprocessor system; (b) a loosely coupled multiprocessor system

two processors of the system takes place by message passing over the communication network.

For a particular processor, its own resources are local, whereas the other processors and their resources are remote. Together, a processor and its resources are usually referred to as a node or site or machine of the distributed computing system.

1.2 EVOLUTION OF DISTRIBUTED COMPUTING SYSTEM

Computer systems are undergoing a revolution. From 1945, when the modem Computer era began, until about 1985, computers were large and expensive. Even minicomputers cost at least tens of thousands of dollars each. As a result, most organizations had only a handful of computers, and for lack of a way to connect them, these operated independently from one another. Starting around the mid-1980s, however, two advances in technology began to change that situation. The first was the development of powerful microprocessors. Initially, these were 8-bit machines, but soon 16-, 32-, and 64-bit CPUs became common.

Many of these had the computing power of a mainframe (i.e., large) computer, but for a fraction of the price. The amount of improvement that has occurred in computer technology in the past half century is truly staggering and totally unprecedented in other industries. From a machine that cost 10 million dollars and executed 1 instruction per second. We have come to machines that cost 1000 dollars and are able to execute 1 billion instructions per second, a price/performance gain of 1013.

The second development was the invention of high-speed computer networks. Local-area networks or LANs allow hundreds of machines within a building to be connected in such a way that small amounts of information can be transferred between machines in a few microseconds or so. Larger amounts of data can be Distributed Computing become popular with the difficulties of centralized processing in mainframe use.

With mainframe software architectures all components are within a central host computer. Users interact with the host through a terminal that captures keystrokes and sends that information to the host. In the last decade however, mainframes have found a new use as a server in distributed client/server architectures (Edelstein 1994). The original PC networks (which have largely superseded mainframes) were based on file sharing architectures, where the server transfers files from a shared location to a desktop environment.

The requested user job is then run (including logic and data) in the desktop environment. File sharing architectures work well if shared usage is low, update contention is low, and the volume of data to be transferred is low. In the 1990s, PC LAN (local area network) computing changed because the capacity of the file sharing was strained as the number of online users grew and graphical user interfaces (GUIs) became popular (making mainframe and terminal displays appear out of date).

The next major step in distributed computing came with separation of software architecture into 2 or 3 tiers. With two tier client-server architectures, the GUI is usually located in the user's desktop environment and the database management services are usually in a server that is a more powerful machine that services many clients.

Processing management is split between the user system interface environment and the database management server environment. The two tier client/server architecture is a good solution for locally distributed computing when work groups are defined as a dozen to 100 people interacting on a LAN simultaneously. However, when the number of users exceeds 100, performance begins to deteriorate and the architecture is also difficult to scale. The three tier architecture (also referred to as the multi-tier architecture) emerged to overcome the limitations of the two tier architecture. In the three tier architecture, a middle tier was added between the user system interface client environment and the database management server environment.

There are a variety of ways of implementing this middle tier, such as transaction processing monitors, messaging middleware, or application servers. The middle tier can perform queuing, application execution, and database queries. For example, if the middle tier provides queuing, the client can deliver its request to the middle layer and disengage because the middle tier will access the data and return the answer to the client. In addition the middle layer adds scheduling and prioritization for work in progress. The three-tier client/server architecture has been shown to improve performance for groups with a large number of users (in the thousands) and improves flexibility when compared to the two tier approach.

Whilst three tier architectures proved successful at separating the logical design of systems, the complexity of collaborating interfaces was still relatively difficult due to technical dependencies between interconnecting processes. Standards for Remote Procedure Calls (RPC) were then used as an attempt to standardise interaction between processes.

As an interface for software to use it is a set of rules for marshalling and un-marshalling parameters and results, a set of rules for encoding and decoding information transmitted between two processes; a few primitive operations to invoke an Individual call, to return its results, and to cancel it; provides provision in the operating system and process structure to maintain and reference state that is shared by the participating processes. RPC requires a communications infrastructure to set up the path between the processes and provide a framework for naming and addressing.

There are two models that provide the framework for using the tools. These are known as the computational model and the interaction model. The computational model describes how a program executes a procedure call when the procedure resides in a different process. The interaction model describes the activities that take place as the call progresses. A marshalling component and a encoding component are brought together by an Interface Definition Language (IDL). An IDL program defines the signatures of RPC operations. The signature is the name of the operation, its input and output parameters, the results it returns and the exceptions it may be asked to handle. RPC has a definite model of a flow of control that passes from a calling process to a called process. The calling process is suspended while the call is in progress and is resumed when the procedure terminates. The procedure may, itself, call other procedures. These can be located anywhere in the systems participating in the application.

1.3 DISTRIBUTED COMPUTING SYSTEM MODELS

Various models are used for building distributed computing systems. These models can be broadly classified into five categories – minicomputer, workstation, workstation-server, processor pool, and hybrid. They are briefly described below.

1.3.1 Minicomputer Model :

The minicomputer model is a simple extension of the centralized time sharing system as shown in Figure 1.2, a distributed computing system based on this model consists of a few minicomputers (they may be large supercomputers as well) interconnected by a communication network. Each minicomputer usually has multiple users simultaneously logged on to it. For this, several interactive terminals are connected to each minicomputer. Each user is logged on to one specific minicomputer, with remote access to other minicomputers. The network allows a user to access remote resources that are available on some machine other than the one on to which the user is currently logged.

The minicomputer model may be used when resource sharing (Such as sharing of information databases of different types, with each type of database located on a different machine) with remote users is desired.

The early ARPAnet is an example of a distributed computing system based on the minicomputer model.

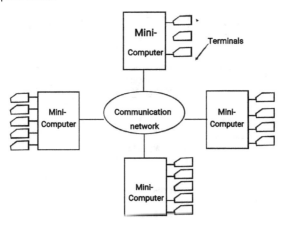

Fig. 1.2 : A distributed computing system based on the minicomputer model

1.3.2 Workstation Model :

As shown in Fig. 1.3, a distributed computing system based on the workstation model consists of several workstations interconnected by a communication network. A company's office or a university department may have several workstations scattered throughout a building or campus, each workstation equipped with its own disk and serving as a single-user computer.

It has been often found that in such an environment, at any one time (especially at night), a significant proportion of the workstations are idle (not being used), resulting in the waste of large amounts of CPU time. Therefore, the idea of the workstation model is to interconnect all these workstations by a high speed LAN so that idle workstations may be used to process jobs of users who are logged onto other workstations and do not have sufficient processing power at their own workstations to get their jobs processed efficiently.

In this model, a user logs onto one of the workstations called his or her "home" workstation and submits jobs for execution. When the system finds that the user's workstation does not have sufficient processing power for executing the processes of the submitted jobs efficiently, it transfers one or more of the process from the user's workstation to some other workstation that is currently idle and gets the process executed there, and finally the result of execution is returned to the user's workstation.

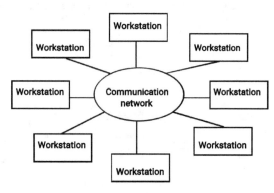

Fig. 1.3 : A distributed computing system based on the workstation model

This model is not so simple to implement as it might appear at first sight because several issues must be resolved. These issues are [Tanenbaum 1995] as follows :

1. How does the system find an idle workstation?

2. How is a process transferred from one workstation to get it executed on another workstation?

3. What happens to a remote process if a user logs onto a workstation that was idle until now and was being used to execute a process of another workstation?

Three commonly used approaches for handling the third issue are as follows:

1. The first approach is to allow the remote process share the resources of the workstation along with its own logged-on user's processes. This method is easy to implement, but it defeats the main idea of workstations serving as personal computers, because if remote processes are allowed to execute simultaneously with the logged on user's own processes, the logged-on user does not get his of her guaranteed response.

2. The second approach is to kill the remote process. The main drawbacks of this method are that all processing done for the remote process gets lost and the file system may be left in an inconsistent state, making this method unattractive.

3. The third approach is to migrate the remote process back to its home workstation, so that its execution can be continued there. This method is difficult to implement because it requires the system to support preemptive process migration facility.

For a number of reasons, such as higher reliability and better scalability, multiple servers are often used for managing the resources of a particular type in a distributed computing system. For example, there may be multiple file servers, each running on a separate minicomputer and cooperating via the network, for managing the files of all the users in the system. Due to this reason, a distinction is often made between the services that are provided to clients and the servers that provide them. That is, a service is an abstract entity that is provided by one or more servers. For example, one or more file servers may be used in a distributed computing system to provide file service to the users.

In this model, a user logs onto a workstation called his or her home workstation. Normal computation activities required by the user's processes are preformed at the user's home workstation, but requests for services provided by special servers (such as a file server or a database server) are sent to a server providing that type of service that performs the user's requested activity and returns the result of request processing to the user's workstation. Therefore, in his model, the user's processes need not be migrated to the server machines for getting the work done by those machines.

For better overall system performance, the local disk of a diskful workstation is normally used for such purposes as storage of temporary files, storage of unshared files, storage of shared files that are rarely changed, paging activity in virtual-memory management, and changing of remotely accessed data.

As compared to the workstation model, the workstation – server model has several advantages:

1. In general, it is much cheaper to use a few minicomputers equipped with large, fast disks that are accessed over the network than a large number of diskful workstations, with each workstation having a small, slow disk.

2. Diskless workstations are also preferred to diskful workstations from a system maintenance point of view. Backup and hardware maintenance are easier to perform with a few large disks than with many small disks scattered all over a building or campus. Furthermore, installing new releases of software (Such as a file server with new functionalities) is easier when the software is to be installed on a few file server machines than on every workstations.

3. In the workstation server model, since all files are managed by the file servers, user have the flexibility to use any workstation and access the files in the same manner irrespective of which workstation the user is currently logged on. Note that this is not true with the workstation model, in which each workstation has its local file system, because different mechanisms are needed to access local and remote files.

4. In the workstation server model, the request response protocol described above is mainly used to access the services of the server machines. Therefore, unlike the workstation model, this model does not need a process migration facility, which is difficult to implement.

The request response protocol is known as the client-server model of communication. In this model, a client process (which in this case resides on a workstation) sends a request to a server process (Which in his case resides on a minicomputer) for getting some service such as a block of a file. The server executes the request and sends back a reply to the client that contains the result of request processing.

The client-server model provides an effective general – purpose approach to the sharing of information and resources in distributed computing systems. It is not only meant for use with the workstation – server model but also can be implemented in a variety of hardware and software environments. The computers used to run the client and server processes need not necessarily be workstations and minicomputers. They can be of many types and there is no need to distinguish between them. It is even possible for both the client and server processes to be run on the same computer. Moreover, some processes are both client and server processes.

That is, a server process may use the services of another server, appearing as a client to the latter.

5. A user has guaranteed response time because workstations are not used for executing remote processes. However, the model does not utilize the processing capability of idle workstations.

1.3.3 Processor Pool Model :

The processor – pool model is based on the observation that most of the time a user does not need any computing power but once in a while he or she may need a very large amount of computing power for a short time. (e.g., when recompiling a program consisting of a large number of files after changing a basic shared declaration). Therefore, unlike the workstation – server model in which a processor is allocated to each user, in the processor-pool model the processors are pooled together to be shared by the users as needed. The pool of processors consists of a large number of microcomputers and minicomputers attached to the network. Each processor in the pool has its own memory to load and run a system program or an application program of the distributed computing system.

As shown in **fig. 1.5**, in the pure processor-pool model, the processors in the pool have no terminals attached directly to them, and users access the system from terminals that are attached to the network via special devices. These terminals are either small diskless workstations or graphic terminals, such as X terminals. A special server (Called a run server) manages and allocates the processors in the pool to different users on a demand basis. When a user submits a job for computation, an appropriate number of processors are temporarily assigned to his or her job by the run server. For example, if the user's computation job is the compilation of a program having n segments, in which each of the segments can be complied independently to produce separate re-locatable object files, n processors from the pool can be allocated to this job to compile all the n segments in parallel. When the computation is completed, the processors are returned to the pool for use by other users.

In the processor-pool model there is no concept of a home machine. That is, a user does not log onto a particular machine but to the system as a whole.

1.3.4 Hybrid Model :

Out of the four models described above, the workstation-server model, is the most widely used model for building distributed computing systems. This is because a large number of computer users only perform simple interactive tasks such as editing jobs, sending electronic mails, and executing small programs. The workstation-server model is ideal for such simple usage. However, in a working environment that has groups of users who often perform jobs needing massive computation, the processor-pool model is more attractive and suitable.

To continue the advantages of both the workstation-server and processor-pool models, a hybrid model may be used to build a distributed computing system.

The hybrid model is based on the workstation-server model but with the addition of a pool of processors. The processors in the pool can be allocated dynamically for computations that are too large for workstations or that requires several computers concurrently for efficient execution. In addition to efficient execution of computation-intensive jobs, the hybrid model gives guaranteed response to interactive jobs by allowing them to be processed on local workstations of the users. However, the hybrid model is more expensive to implement than the workstation – server model or the processor-pool model.

2

ISSUES IN DESIGNING A DISTRIBUTED OPERATING SYSTEM

2.1 ISSUES IN DESIGNING A DISTRIBUTED OPERATING SYSTEM

In general, designing a distributed operating system is more difficult than designing a centralized operating system for several reasons. In the design of a centralized operating system, it is assumed that the operating system has access to complete and accurate information about the environment in which it is functioning. For example, a centralized operating system can request status information, being assured that the interrogated component will not charge state while awaiting a decision based on that status information, since only the single operating system asking the question may give commands. However, a distributed operating system must be designed with the assumption that complete information about the system environment will never be available. In a distributed system, the resources are physically separated, there is no common clock among the multiple processors, delivery of messages is delayed, and messages could even be lost. Due to all these reasons, a distributed operating system does not have up-to-date, consistent knowledge about the state of the various components of the underlying distributed system. Obviously, lack of up-to-date and consistent information makes many things (Such as management of resources and synchronization of cooperating activities) much harder in the design of a distributed operating system. For example, it is hard to schedule the processors optimally if the operation system is not sure how many of them are up at the moment.

Despite these complexities and difficulties, a distributed operating system must be designed to provide all the advantages of a distributed system to its users. That is, the users should be able to view a distributed system as a virtual centralized system that is flexible, efficient, reliable, secure and easy to use. To meet this challenge, the designers of a distributed operating system must deal with several design issues.

2.2 TRANSPARENCY

A distributed system that is able to present itself to user and application as if it were only a single computer system is said to be transparent. There are eight types of transparencies in a distributed system:

Access Transparency: It hides differences in data representation and how a resource is accessed by a user. Example, a distributed system may have a computer system that runs different operating systems, each having their own file naming conventions. Differences in naming conventions as well as how files can be manipulated should be hidden from the users and applications.

Location Transparency: Hides where exactly the resource is located physically. Example, by assigning logical names to resources like yahoo.com, one cannot get an idea of the location of the web page's main server.

Migration Transparency: Distributed system in which resources can be moved without affecting how the resource can be accessed are said to provide migration transparency. It hides that the resource may move from one location to another.

Relocation Transparency: this transparency deals with the fact that resources can be relocated while it is being accessed without the user who is using the application to know anything. Example: using a Wi-Fi system on laptops while moving from place to place without getting disconnected.

Replication Transparency: Hides the fact that multiple copies of a resource could exist simultaneously. To hide replication, it is essential that the replicas have the same name. Consequently, as system that supports replication should also support location transparency.

Concurrency Transparency: It hides the fact that the resource may be shared by several competitive users. Example, two independent users may each have stored their file on the same server and may be accessing the same table in a shared database. In such cases, it is important that each user doesn't notice that the others are making use of the same resource.

Failure Transparency: Hides failure and recovery of the resources. It is the most difficult task of a distributed system and is even impossible when certain apparently realistic assumptions are made. Example: A user cannot distinguish between a very slow or dead resource. Same error message come when a server is down or when the network is overloaded of when the connection from the client side is lost. So here, the user is unable to understand what has to be done, either the user should wait for the network to clear up, or try again later when the server is working again.

Persistence Transparency: It hides if the resource is in memory or disk. Example, Object oriented database provides facilities for directly invoking methods on storage objects. First the database server copies the object states from the disk i.e. main memory performs the operation and writes the state back to the disk. The user does not know that the server is moving between primary and secondary memory.

Persistence Transparency	Hide whether a (software) resource is in memory or on disk Description
Access Location	Hide differences in data representation and how a resource is accessed Hide where a resource is located
Migration Relocation Replication Concurrency Failure	Hide that a resource may move to another location Hide that a resource may be moved to another location while in use Hide that a resource may be shared by several competitive users Hide that a resource may be shared by several competitive users Hide the failure and recovery of a resource

Summary of the transparencies

In a distributed system, multiple users who are spatially separated use the system concurrently. In such a duration, it is economical to share the system resources (hardware or software) among the concurrently executing user processes. However since the number of available resources in a computing system is restricted, one user process must necessarily influence the action of other concurrently executing user processes, as it competes for resources. For example, concurrent updates to the same file by two different processes should be prevented. Concurrency transparency means that each user has a feeling that he or she is the sole user of the system and other users do not exist in the system. For providing concurrency transparency, the resource sharing mechanisms of the distributed operating system must have the following four properties :

> An event-ordering property ensures that all access requests to various system resources are properly ordered to provide a consistent view to all users of the system.

> A mutual-exclusion property ensures that at any time at most one process accesses a shared resource, which must not be used simultaneously by multiple processes if program operation is to be correct.

> A no-starvation property ensures that if every process that is granted a resource, which must not be used simultaneously by multiple processes, eventually releases it, every request for that resource is eventually granted.

> A no-deadlock property ensures that a situation will never occur in which competing processes prevent their mutual progress even though no single one requests more resources than available in the system.

2.3 PERFORMANCE TRANSPARENCY

The aim of performance transparency is to allow the system to be automatically reconfigured to improve performance, as loads vary dynamically in the system. As far as practicable, a situation in which one processor of the system is overloaded with jobs while another processor is idle should not be allowed to occur. That is, the processing capability of the system should be uniformly distributed among the currently available jobs in the system.

This requirements calls for the support of intelligent resource allocation and process migration facilities in distributed operating systems.

2.4 SCALING TRANSPARENCY

The aim of scaling transparency is to allow the system to expand in scale without disrupting the activities of the users. This requirement calls for open-system architecture and the use of scalable algorithms for designing the distributed operating system components.

2.5 RELIABILITY

In general, distributed systems are expected to be more reliable than centralized systems due to the existence of multiple instances of resources. However, the existence of multiple instances of the resources alone cannot increase the system's reliability. Rather, the distributed operating system, which manages these resources must be designed properly to increase the system's reliability by taking full advantage of this characteristic feature of a distributed system.

A fault is a mechanical or algorithmic defect that may generate an error. A fault in a system causes system failure. Depending on the manner in which a failed system behaves, system failures are of two types – fail stop [Schlichting and Schneider 1983] and Byzantine [Lamport et al. 1982]. In the case of fail-step failure, the system stops functioning after changing to a state in which its failure can be detected. On the other hand, in the case of Byzantine failure, the system continues to function but produces wrong results. Undetected software bugs often cause Byzantine failure of a system. Obviously, Byzantine failures are much more difficult to deal with than fail-stop failures.

For higher reliability, the fault-handling mechanisms of a distributed operating system must be designed properly to avoid faults, to tolerate faults, and to detect and recover form faults. Commonly used methods for dealing with these issues are briefly described text.

2.6 FAULT AVOIDANCE

Fault avoidance deals with designing the components of the system in such a way that the occurrence of faults in minimized. Conservative design practice such as using high reliability components are often employed for improving the system's reliability based on the idea of fault avoidance. Although a distributed operating system often has little or no role to play in improving the fault avoidance capability of a hardware component, the designers of the various software components of the distributed operating system must test them thoroughly to make these components highly reliable.

2.7 FAULT TOLERANCE

Fault tolerance is the ability of a system to continue functioning in the event of partial system failure. The performance of the system might be degraded due to partial failure, but otherwise the system functions properly. Some of the important concepts that may be used to improve the fault tolerance ability of a distributed operating system are as follows :

1. **Redundancy techniques :** The basic idea behind redundancy techniques is to avoid single points of failure by replicating critical hardware and software components, so that if one of them fails, the others can be used to continue. Obviously, having two or more copies of a critical component makes it possible, at least in principle, to continue operations in spite of occasional partial failures. For example, a critical process can be simultaneously executed on two nodes so that if one of the two nodes fails, the execution of the process can be completed at the other node. Similarly, a critical file may be replicated on two or more storage devices for better reliability.

   Notice that with redundancy techniques additional system overhead is needed to maintain two or more copies of a replicated resource and to keep all the copies of a resource consistent. For example, if a file is replicated on two or more nodes of a distributed system, additional disk storage space is required and for correct functioning, it is often necessary that all the copies of the file are mutually consistent. In general, the larger is the number of copies kept, the better is the reliability but the incurred overhead involved. Therefore, a distributed operating system must be designed to maintain a proper balance between the degree of reliability and the incurred overhead. This raises an important question : How much replication is enough? For an answer to this question, note that a system is said to be k-fault tolerant if it can continue to function even in the event of the failure of k components [Cristian 1991, Nelson 1990]. Therefore, if the system is to be designed to tolerance k fail − stop failures, $k + 1$ replicas are needed.

If k replicas are lost due to failures, the remaining one replica can be used for continued functioning of the system. On the other hand, if the system is to be designed to tolerance k Byzantine failures, a minimum of $2k + 1$ replicas are needed. This is because a voting mechanism can be used to believe the majority $k + 1$ of the replicas when k replicas behave abnormally.

Another application of redundancy technique is in the design of a stable storage device, which is a virtual storage device that can even withstand transient I/O faults and decay of the storage media. The reliability of a critical file may be improved by storing it on a stable storage device.

2. **Distributed control:** For better reliability, many of the particular algorithms or protocols used in a distributed operating system must employ a distributed control mechanism to avoid single points of failure. For example, a highly available distributed file system should have multiple and independent file servers controlling multiple and independent storage devices. In addition to file servers, a distributed control technique could also be used for name servers, scheduling algorithms, and other executive control functions. It is important to note here that when multiple distributed servers are used in a distributed system to provide a particular type of service, the servers must be independent. That is, the design must not require simultaneous functioning of the servers; otherwise, the reliability will become worse instead of getting better. Distributed control mechanisms are described throughout this book.

2.8 FAULT DETECTION AND RECOVERY

The faulty detection and recovery method of improving reliability deals with the use of hardware and software mechanisms to determine the occurrence of a failure and then to correct the system to a state acceptable for continued operation. Some of the commonly used techniques for implementing this method in a distributed operating system are as follows.

1. **Atomic transactions :** An atomic transaction (or just transaction for shore) is a computation consisting of a collection of operation that take place indivisibly in the presence of failures and concurrent computations. That is, either all of the operations are performed successfully or none of their effects prevails, other processes executing concurrently cannot modify or observe intermediate states of the computation. Transactions help to preserve the consistency of a set of shared date objects (e.g. files) in the face of failures and concurrent access. They make crash recovery much easier, because transactions can only end in two states : Either all the operations of the transaction are performed or none of the operations of the transaction is performed.

In a system with transaction facility, if a process halts unexpectedly due to a hardware error before a transaction is completed, the system subsequently restores any data objects that were undergoing modification to their original states. Notice that if a system does not support a transaction mechanism, unexpected failure of a process during the processing of an operation may leave the data objects that were undergoing modification in an inconsistent state. Therefore, without transaction facility, it may be difficult or even impossible in some cases to roll back (recover) the data objects from their current inconsistent states to their original states.

2. **Stateless servers:** The client-server model is frequently used in distributed systems to service user requests. In this model, a server may be implemented by using any one of the following two service paradigms – stateful or stateless. The two paradigms are distinguished by one aspect of the client – server relationship, whether or not the history of the serviced requests between a client and a server affects the execution of the next service request. The stateful approach does depend on the history of the serviced requests, but the stateless approach does not depend on it. Stateless servers have a distinct advantage over stateful servers in the event of a failure. That is, the stateless service paradigm makes crash recovery very easy because no client state information is maintained by the server. On the other hand, the stateful service paradigm requires complex crash recovery procedures. Both the client and server need to reliably detect crashes. The server needs to detect client crashes so that it can discard any state it is holding for the client, and the client must detect server crashes so that it can perform necessary error – handling activities. Although stateful service becomes necessary in some cases, to simplify the failure detection and recovery actions, the stateless service paradigm must be used, wherever possible.

3. **Acknowledgments** and timeout-based retransmission of messages. In a distributed system, events such as a node crash or a communication link failure may interrupt a communication that was in progress between two processes, resulting in the loss of a message. Therefore, a reliable interprocess communication mechanism must have ways to detect lost messages so that they can be retransmitted. Handling of lost messages usually involves return of acknowledgment messages and retransmissions on the basis of timeouts. That is, the receiver must return an acknowledgment message for every message received, and if the sender does not receive any acknowledgement for a message within a fixed timeout period, it assumes that the message was lost and retransmits the message. A problem associated with this approach is that of duplicate message.

Duplicates messages may be sent in the event of failures or because of timeouts. Therefore, a reliable interprocess communication mechanism should also be capable of detecting and handling duplicate messages. Handling of duplicate messages usually involves a mechanism for automatically generating and assigning
appropriate sequence numbers to messages. Use of acknowledgement messages, timeout-based retransmissions of messages, and handling of duplicate request messages for reliable communication.

The mechanisms described above may be employed to create a very reliable distributed system. However, the main drawback of increased system reliability is potential loss of execution time efficiency due to the extra overhead involved in these techniques. For many systems it is just too costly to incorporate a large number of reliability mechanisms. Therefore, the major challenge for distributed operating system designers is to integrate these mechanisms in a cost-effective manner for producing a reliable system.

2.9 FLEXIBILITY

Another important issue in the design of distributed operating systems is flexibility. Flexibility is the most important features for open distributed systems. The design of a distributed operating system should be flexible due to the following reasons :

> **1. Ease of modification :** From the experience of system designers, it has been found that some parts of the design often need to be replaced / modified either because some bug is detected in the design or because the design is no longer suitable for the changed system environment or new-user requirements. Therefore, it should be easy to incorporate changes in the system in a user-transparent manner or with minimum interruption caused to the users.

> **2. Ease of enhancement :** In every system, new functionalities have to be added from time to time it more powerful and easy to use. Therefore, it should be easy to add new services to the system. Furthermore, if a group of users do not like the style in which a particular service is provided by the operating system, they should have the flexibility to add and use their own service that works in the style with which the users of that group are more familiar and feel more comfortable.

The most important design factor that influences the flexibility of a distributed operating system is the model used for designing its kernel. The kernel of an operating system is its central controlling part that provides basic system facilities. It operates in a separate address space that is inaccessible to user processes. It is the only part of an operating system that a user cannot replace or modify. We saw that in the case of a distributed operating system identical kernels are run on all the nodes of the distributed system.

The two commonly used models for kernel design in distributed operating systems are the monolithic kernel and the microkernel. In the monolithic kernel model, most operating system services such as process management, memory management, device management, file management, name management, and inter-process communication are provided by the kernel. As a result, the kernel has a large, monolithic structure. Many distributed operating systems that are extensions or limitations of the UNIX operating system use the monolithic kernel model. This is mainly because UNIX itself has a large, monolithic kernel.

On the other hand, in the microkernel model, the main goal is to keep the kernel as small as possible. Therefore, in this model, the kernel is a very small nucleus of software that provides only the minimal facilities necessary for implementing additional operating system services. The only services provided by the kernel in this model are inter-process communication low level device management, a limited amount of low-level process management and some memory management. All other operating system services, such as file management, name management, additional process, and memory management activities and much system call handling are implemented as user-level server processes. Each server process has its own address space and can be programmed separately.

As compared to the monolithic kernel model, the microkernel model has several advantages. In the monolithic kernel model, the large size of the kernel reduces the overall flexibility and configurability of the resulting operating system. On the other hand, the resulting operating system of the microkernel model is highly modular in nature. Due to this characteristic feature, the operating system of the microkernel model is easy to design, implement, and install. Moreover, since most of the services are implemented as user-level server processes, it is also easy to modify the design or add new services.

In spite of its potential performance cost, the microkernel model is being preferred for the design of modern distributed operating systems. The two main reasons for this are as follows.

1. The advantages of the microkernel model more than compensate for the performance cost. Notice that the situation here is very similar to the one that caused high level programming languages to be preferred to assembly languages. In spite of the better performance of programs written in assembly languages, most programs are written in high-level languages due to the advantages of ease of design, maintenance, and portability. Similarly, the flexibility advantages of the microkernel model previously described more than outweigh its small performance penalty.

2. Some experimental results have shown that although in theory the microkernel model seems to have poorer performance than the monolithic kernel model, this is not true in practice. This is because other factors tend to dominate, and the small overhead involved in exchanging messages is usually negligible.

2.10 PERFORMANCE

If a distributed system is to be used its performance must be at least as good as a centralized system. That is, when a particular application is run on a distributed system, its overall performance should be better than or at least equal to that of running the same application on a single processor system. However, to achieve his goal, it is important that the various components of the operating system of a distributed system be designed properly; otherwise, the overall performance of the distributed system may turn out to be worse than a centralized system. Some design principles considered useful for better performance are as follows :

1. Batch if possible, Batching often helps in improving performance greatly. For example, transfer of data across the network in large chunks rather than as individual pages is much more efficient. Similarly, piggybacking of acknowledgement of previous messages with the next message during a series of messages exchanged between two communicating entities also improves performance.

2. Cache whenever possible : Caching of data at clients' sites frequently improves overall system performance because it makes data available wherever it is being currently used, thus saving a large amount of computing time and network bandwidth. In addition, caching reduces contention on centralized resources.

3. Minimize copying of data : Data copying overhead (e.g. moving data in and out of buffers) involves a substantial CPU cost of many operations. For example, while being transferred from its sender to its receiver, a message data may take the following path on the sending side :

a) From sender's stack to its message buffer

b) From the message buffer in the sender's address space to the message buffer in the kernel's address space

c) Finally, from the kernel to the network interface board

On the receiving side, the data probably takes a similar path in the reverse direction. Therefore, in this case, a total of six copy operations are involved in the message transfer operation. Similarly, in several systems, the data copying overhead is also large for read and write operations on block I/O devices. Therefore, for better performance, it is desirable to avoid copying of data, although this is not always simple to achieve. Making optimal use of memory management often helps in eliminating much data movement between the kernel, block I/O devices, clients, and servers.

4. Minimize network traffic : System performance may also be improved by reducing internode communication costs. For example, accesses to remote resources require communication, possibly through intermediate nodes. Therefore, migrating a process closer to the resources it is using most heavily may be helpful in reducing network traffic in the system if the decreased cost of accessing its favorite resource offsets the possible increased post of accessing its less favored ones. Another way to reduce network traffic is to use the process migration facility to cluster two or more processes that frequently communicate with each other on the same node of the system. Avoiding the collection of global state information for making some decision also helps in reducing network traffic.

5. Take advantage of fine-grain parallelism for multiprocessing. Performance can also be improved by taking advantage of fine-giam parallelism for multiprocessing. For example, threads are often used for structuring server processes. Servers structured as a group of threads can operate efficiently, because they can simultaneously service requests from several clients. Fine-grained concurrency control of simultaneous accesses by multiple processes, to a shared resource is another example of application of this principle for better performance.

Throughout the book we will come across the use of these design principles in the design of the various distributed operating system components.

2.11 SCALABILITY

Scalability refers to the capability of a system to adapt to increased service load. It is inevitable that a distributed system will grow with time since it is very common to add new machines or an entire subnetwork to the system to take care of increased workload or organizational changes in a company. Therefore, a distributed operating system should be designed to easily cope with the growth of nodes and users in the system. That is, such growth should not cause serious disruption of service or significant loss of performance to users. Some guiding principles for designing scalable distributed systems are as follows :

> **1. Avoid centralized entities :** In the design of a distributed operating system, use of centralized entities such as a single central file server or a single database for the entire system makes the distributed system non-scalable due to the following reasons :

Security :

In order that the users can trust the system and rely on it, the various resources of a computer system must be protected against destruction and unauthorized access. Enforcing security in a distributed system is more difficult than in a centralized system because of the lack of a single point of control and the use of insecure networks for data communication. In a centralized system, all users are authenticated by the system at login time, and the system can easily check whether a user is authorized to perform the requested operation on an accessed resource. In a distributed system, however, since the client – server model is often used for requesting and providing services, when a client sends a request message to a server, the server must have some way of knowing who is the client. This is not so simple as it might appear because any client identification field in the message cannot be trusted. This is because an intruder (a person or program trying to obtain unauthorized access to system resources) may pretend to be an authorized client or may change the message contents during transmission. Therefore, as compared to a centralized system, enforcement of security in a distributed system has the following additional requirements :

1. It should be possible for the sender of a message to know that the message was received by the intended receiver.

2. It should be possible for the receiver of a message to know that the message was sent by the genuine sender.

3. It should be possible for both the sender and receiver of a message to be guaranteed that the contents of the message were not changed while it was in transfer.

Cryptography is the only known practical method for dealing with these security aspects of a distributed system. In this method comprehension of private information is prevented by encrypting the information, which can then be decrypted only by authorized users.

Another guiding principle for security is that a system whose security depends on the integrity of the fewest possible entities is more likely to remain secure as it grows. For example, it is much simpler to ensure security based on the integrity of the much smaller number of servers rather than trusting thousands of clients. In this case, it is sufficient to only ensure the physical security of these servers and the software they run.

REMOTE PROCEDURE CALLS

3.1 INTRODUCTION TO RPC

A remote procedure call (RPC) is an inter-process communication that allows a computer program to cause a procedure to execute in another address space (commonly on another computer on a shared network) without the programmer explicitly coding the details for this remote interaction.

It further aims at hiding most of the intricacies of message passing and is idle for client-server application.

RPC allows programs to call procedures located on other machines. But the procedures 'send' and 'receive' do not conceal the communication which leads to achieving access transparence in distributed systems.

Example: when process A calls a procedure on B, the calling process on A is suspended and the execution of the called procedure takes place. (PS: function, method, procedure difference, stub, 5 state process model definition)

Information can be transported in the form of parameters and can come back in procedure result. No message passing is visible to the programmer. As calling and called procedures exist on different machines, they execute in different address spaces, the parameters and result should be identical and if machines crash during communication, it causes problems.

3.1.1 RPC Operations:

1) **Conventional procedure call**

   For a call of a program, an empty stack is present to make the call, the caller pushes the parameters onto the stack (last one first order). After the read has finished running, it puts the return values in a register and removes the return address and transfers controls back to the caller. Parameters can be called by value or reference.

   a) *Call by Value:* Here the parameters are copied into the stack. The value parameter is just an initialized local variable. The called procedure may modify the variable, but such changes do not affect the original value at the calling side.

   b) *Call by reference:* It is a pointer to the variable. In the call to Read, the second parameter is a reference parameter. It does not modify the array in the calling procedure.

   c) *Call-by-copy:* Another parameter passing mechanism exists along with the above two, its called call-by-copy or *Restore*. Here the caller copies the variable to the stack and then copies the variable to the stack and then copies it back after the call, overwriting the caller's original values. The decision of which parameter passing mechanism to use is normally made by the language designers and is a fixed property of the language. Sometimes it depends on the data type being passed.

2. Client and Server Stubs

A *stub* in distributed computing is a piece of code used for converting parameters passed during a Remote Procedure Call.

The main idea of an RPC is to allow a local computer (client) to remotely call procedures on a remote computer (server). The client and server use different address spaces, so conversion of parameters used in a function call have to be performed; otherwise the values of those parameters could not be used, because of pointers to the computer's memory pointing to different data on each machine.

The client and server may also use different data representations even for simple parameters. Stubs are used to perform the conversion of the parameters, so a Remote Function Call looks like a local function call for the remote computer.

For transparency of RPC, the calling procedure should not know that the called procedure is executing on a different machine.

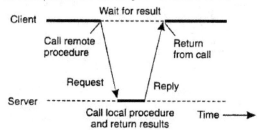

Figure 3.1: Principle of RPC between a client and server program.

Client Stub: Used when read is a remote procedure. Client stub is put into a library and is called using a calling sequence. It calls for the local operating system. It does not ask for the local operating system to give data, it asks the server and then blocks itself till the reply comes.

Server Stub: when a message arrives, it directly goes to the server stub. Server stub has the same functions as the client stub. The stub here unpacks the parameters from the message and then calls the server procedure in the usual way.

Summary of the process:

1. The client procedure calls the client stub in the normal way.
2. The client stub builds a message and calls the local operating system.
3. The client's as sends the message to the remote as.
4. The remote as gives the message to the server stub.
5. The server stub unpacks the parameters and calls the server.
6. The server does the work and returns the result to the stub.
7. The server stub packs it in a message and calls its local as.
8. The server's as sends the message to the client's as.
9. The client's as gives the message to the client stub.
10. The stub unpacks the result and returns to the client.

3.2 TRANSPARENCY OF RPC

A major issue in the design of an RPC facility is its transparency property. A transparent RPC mechanism is one in which local procedures and remote procedures are (effectively) indistinguishable to programmers. This requires the following two types of transparencies:

1. Syntactic transparency means that a remote procedures call should have exactly the same syntax as a local procedure call.

2. Semantic transparency means that the semantics of a remote procedure call are identical to those of a local procedure call.

It is not very difficult to achieve syntactic transparency of an RPC mechanism, and we have seen that the semantics of remote procedure calls are also analogous to that of local procedure calls for most parts :

The calling process is suspended until the called procedure returns.
The caller can pass arguments to the called procedure (remote procedure).
The called procedure (remote procedure) can return results to the caller.

Unfortunately, achieving exactly the same semantics for remote procedure calls as for local procedure calls is close to impossible. This is mainly because of the following differences between remote procedure calls and local procedure calls.

1. Unlike local procedure calls, with remote procedure calls the called procedure is executed in an address space that is disjoint from the calling program's address space. Due to this reason, the called (remote) procedure cannot have access to any variables or data values in the calling program's environment.

Thus in the absence of shared memory, it is meaningless to pass addresses in arguments, making call-by-reference pointers highly unattractive. Similarly, it is meaningless to pass argument values containing pointer structures (e.g., linked lists), since pointers are normally represented by memory addresses.

According to Bal et al. [1989] dereferencing a pointer passed by the caller has to be done at the caller's side, which implies extra communication. An alternative implementation is to send a copy of the value pointed at the receiver, but this has subtly different semantics and may be difficult to implement if the pointer points into the middle of a complex data structure, such as a directed graph. Similarly, call by reference can be replaced by copy in / copy out, but at the cost of slightly different semantics.

2. Remote procedure calls are more vulnerable to failure than local procedure calls, since they involve two different processes and possibly a network and two different computers. Therefore programs that make use of remote procedure calls must have the capability of handling even those errors that cannot occur in local procedure calls. The need for the ability to take care of the possibility of processor crashes and communication problems of a network makes it even more difficult to obtain the same semantics for remote procedure calls as for local procedure calls.

3. Remote procedure calls consume much more time (100 – 1000 times more) than local procedure calls. This is mainly due to the involvement of a communication network in RPCs. Therefore applications using RPCs must also have the capability to handle the long delays that may possibly occur due to network congestion.

Because of these difficulties in achieving normal call semantics for remote procedure calls, some researchers feel that the RPC facility should be nontransparent. For example, Hamilton [1984] argues that remote procedures should be treated differently from local procedures from the start, resulting in a nontransparent RPC mechanism. Similarly, the designers of RPC were of the opinion that although the RPC system should hide low-level details of message passing from the users, failures and long delays should not be hidden from the caller. That is, the caller should have the flexibility of handling failures and long delays in an application – dependent manner. In conclusion, although in most environments total semantic transparency is impossible, enough can be done to ensure that distributed application programmers feel comfortable.

3.3 IMPLEMENTING RPC MECHANISM

To achieve the goal of semantic transparency, the implementation of an RPC mechanism is based on the concept of stubs, which provide a perfectly normal (local) procedure call abstraction by concealing from programs the interface to the underlying RPC system. We saw that an RPC involves a client process and a server process. Therefore, to conceal the interface of the underlying RPC system from both the client and server processes, a separate stub procedure is associated with each of the two processes. Moreover, to hide the existence and functional details of the underlying network, an RPC communication package (known as RPCRuntime) is used on both the client and server sides. Thus, implementation of an RPC mechanism usually involves the following five elements of program [Birrell and Nelson 1984].

1. The client
2. The client stub
3. The RPCRuntime
4. The server stub
5. The server

The interaction between them is shown in Figure 4.2. The client, the client stub, and one instance of RPCRuntime execute on the client machine, while the server, the server stub, and another instance of RPCRuntime execute on the server machine. The job of each of these elements is described below

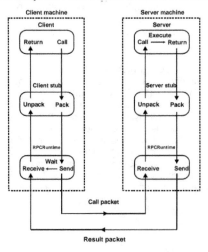

Fig. 3.2 : Implementation of RPC mechanism

Client :

The client is a user process that initiates a remote procedure call. To make a remote procedure call, the client makes a perfectly normal local call that invokes a corresponding procedure in the client stub.

Client Stub :

The client stub is responsible for carrying out the following two tasks :

*) On receipt of a call request from the client, it packs a specification of the target procedure and the arguments into a message and then asks the local RPCRuntime to send it to the server stub.

*) On receipt of the result of procedure execution, it unpacks the result and passes it to the client.

RPCRuntime :

The RPCRuntime handles transmission of messages across the network between client and server machines. It is responsible for retransmissions, acknowledgements, packet routing, and encryption. The RPCRuntime on the client machine receives the call request message from the client stub and sends it to the server machine. It also receives the message containing the result of procedure execution from the server machine and passes it to the client stub.

On the other hand, the RPCRuntime on the server machine receives the message containing the result of procedure execution from the server stub and sends it to the client machine. It also receives the call request message from the client machine and passes it to the server stub.

Server Stub :

The job of the server stub is very similar to that of the client stub. It performs the following two tasks :

*) On the receipt of the call request message from the local RPCRuntime, the server stub unpacks it and makes a perfectly normal call to invoke the appropriate procedure in the server.

*) On receipt of the result of procedure execution from the server, the server stub packs the result into a message and then asks the local RPCRuntime to send it to the client stub.

Server :

On receiving a call request from the server stub, the server executes the appropriate procedure and returns the result of procedure execution to the server stub.

Note here that the beauty of the whole scheme is the total ignorance on the part of the client that the work was done remotely instead of by the local kernel. When the client gets control following the procedure call that it made, all it knows is that the results of the procedure execution are available to it. Therefore, as far as the client is concerned, remote services are accessed by making ordinary (local) procedure calls, not by using the send and receive primitives. All the details of the message passing are hidden in the client and server stubs, making the steps involved in message passing invisible to both the client and the server.

3.4 STUB GENERATION

Stubs can be generated in one of the following two ways :

> **1. Manually :** In this method, the RPC implementor provides a set of translation functions from which a user can construct his or her own stubs. This method is simple to implement and can handle very complex parameter types.

> **2. Automatically :** This is the more commonly used method for stub generation. It uses Interface Definition Language (IDL) that is used to define the interface between a client and a server. An interface definition is mainly a list of procedure names supported by the interface, together with the types of their arguments and results. This is sufficient information for the client and server to independently perform compile-time type checking and to generate appropriate calling sequences. However, an interface definition also contains other information that helps RPC reduce data storage and the amount of data transferred over the network. For example, an interface definition has information to indicate whether each argument is input, output, or both – only input arguments need be copied from client to server and only output arguments need be copied from server to client. Similarly, an interface definition also has information about type definitions, enumerated types, and defined constants that each side uses to manipulate data from RPC calls making it unnecessary for both the client and the server to store this information separately.

A server program that implements procedures in an interface is said to export the interface and a client program that calls procedures from an interface is said to import the interface. When writing a distributed application, a programmer first writes an interface definition using the IDL. He or she can then write the client program that imports the interface and the server program that exports the interface. The interface definition is processed using an IDL computer to generate components that can be combined with client and server programs, without making any changes to the existing compliers. In particular, from an interface definition, an IDL complier generate a client stub procedure and a server such procedure for each procedure is the interface, the appropriate marshaling and un-marshaling operations (described later in this chapter) in each stub procedure, and a header file that supports the data types in the interface definition.

The header file is included in the source files of both the client and server programs, the client stub procedures are complied and linked with the client program, and the server stub procedures are compiled and linked with the server program. An IDL compiler an be designed to process interface definitions for use with different languages, enabling clients and servers written in different languages, to communicate by using remote procedure calls.

3.5 RPC MESSAGES

Any remote procedure call involves a client process and a server process that are possibly located on different computers. The mode of interaction between the client and server is that the client asks the server to execute a remote procedure and the server returns the result of execution of the concerned procedure to the client. Based on this mode of interaction, the two types of messages involved in the implementation of an RPC system are as follows :

1. Call messages that are sent by the client to the server for requesting execution of a particular remote procedure.

2. Reply messages that are sent by the server to the client for returning the result of remote procedure execution.

The protocol of the concerned RPC system defines the format of these two types of message. Normally, an RPC protocol is independent of transport protocols. That is, RPC does not care how a message is passed from one process to another. Therefore an RPC protocol deals only with the specification and interpretation of these two types of messages.

Call Messages :

Since a call message is used to request execution of a particular remote procedure the two basic components necessary in a call message are as follows :
1. The identification information of the remote procedure to be executed.
2. The arguments necessary for the execution of the procedure.

In addition to these two fields, a call message normally has the following fields.

3. A message identification field that consists of a sequence number. This field is useful of two ways – for identifying lost
messages and duplicate messages in case of system failures and for properly matching reply messages to outstanding call messages, especially in those cases when the replies of several outstanding call messages arrive out of order.

4. A message type field that is used to distinguish call messages

from reply messages. For example, in an RPC system, this field may be set to 0 for all call messages and set to 1 for all reply messages.

5. A client identification field that may be used for two purposes – to allow the server of the RPC to identify the client to whom the reply message has to be returned and to allow the server to check the authentication of the client process for executing the concerned procedure.

Thus, a typical RPC all message format may be of the form shown in Figure 3.2.

Reply Messages :

When the server of an RPC receives a call message from a client, it could be faced with one of the following conditions. In the list below, it is assumed for a particular condition that no problem was detected by the server for any of the previously listed conditions :

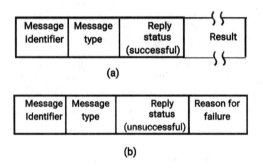

(a)

Message Identifier	Message type	Reply status (unsuccessful)	Reason for failure

(b)

Fig. 3.3 A typical RPC reply message format :
(a) a successful reply message format;
(b) an unsuccessful reply message format

3.6 MARSHALING ARGUMENTS AND RESULTS

Implementation of remote procedure calls involves the transfer of arguments from the client process to the server process and the transfer of results from the server process to the client process. These arguments and results are basically language-level data structures (program objects), which are transferred in the form of message data between the two computers involved in the call. The transfer of message data between two computers requires encoding and decoding of the message data. For RPC this operation is known as marshaling and basically involves the following actions.

1. Taking the arguments (of a client process) or the result (of a server process) that will form the message data to be set to the remote process.

2. Encoding the message data of step 1 above on the sender's computer. This encoding process involves the conversion of program objects into a stream form that is suitable for transmission and placing them into a message buffer.

3. Decoding of the message data on the receiver's computer. This decoding process involves the reconstruction of program objects from the message data that was received in stream form.

In order that encoding and decoding of an RPC message can be performed successfully, the order and the representation method (tagged or untagged) used to marshal arguments and results must be known to both the client and the server of the RPC. This provides a degree of type safety between a client a server because the server will not accept a call from a client until the client uses the same interface definition as the server. Type safety is of particular importance to servers since it allows them to survive against corrupt call requests.

The marshaling process must reflect the structure of all types of program objects used in the concerned language. These include primitive types, structured types, and user defined types. Marshaling procedures may be classified into two groups :

1. Those provided as a part of the RPC software. Normally marshaling procedures for scalar data types, together with procedures to marshal compound types built from the scalar ones, fall in this group.

2. Those that are defined by the users of the RPC system. This group contains marshaling procedures for user – defined data types and data types that include pointers. For example, in Concurrent CLU, developed for use in the Cambridge Distributed Computer System, for user-defined types, the type definition must contain procedures for marshaling.

A good RPC system should always generate in-line marshaling code for every remote call so that the users are relieved of the burden of writing their own marshaling procedures. However, practically it is difficult to achieve this goal because of the unacceptable large amounts of code that may have to be generated for handling all possible data types.

3.7 SERVER MANAGEMENT

In RPC based applications, two important issues that need to be considered for every management are server implementation and server creation.

Server Implementation :

Based on the style of implementation used, servers may be of two types : stateful and stateless.

Stateful Servers :

A stateful server maintains clients' state information from one remote procedure call to the next. That is, in case of two subsequent calls by a client to a stateful server, some state information pertaining to the service performed for the client as a result of the first call execution is stored by the server process. These clients' state information is subsequently used at the time of executing the second call.

For example, let us consider a server for byte-stream files that allows the following operations on files :

Open (filename, mode) :

This operation is used to open a file identified by filename in the specified mode. When the server executes this operation, it creates an entry for this file in a file-table that it uses for maintaining the file state information of all the open files. The file state information normally consists of the identifier of the file, the open mode, and the current position of a nonnegative integer pointer, called the read write pointer. When a file is opened, its read-write pointer is set to zero and the server returns to the client a file identifier (fid), which is used by the client for subsequent accesses to that file.

Read (fid, n, buffer) :

This operation is used to get n bytes of data from the file identified by fid into the buffer named buffer. When the server executes this operation, it returns to the client n bytes of file data starting from the byte currently addressed by the read − write pointer and then increments the read − write pointer by n.

Write (fid, n, buffer) :

On execution of this operation, the server takes n bytes of data from the specified buffer, writes it into the file identified by fid at the byte position currently addressed by the read − write pointer, and then increments the read − write pointer by n.

Seek (fid, position) :

This operation causes the server to change the value of the read write pointer of the file identified by fid to the new value specified as position.

Close (fid) :

This statement causes the server to delete from its file table the file state information of the file identified by fid.

The file server mentioned above is stateful because it maintains the current state information for a file that has been opened for use by a client. Therefore, as shown in Fig. 3.3, after opening a file, if a client makes two subsequent Read (fig, 100, buf), calls, the first call will return the first 100 bytes (bytes 0 – 99) and the second call will return the next 100 bytes (bytes 100 – 199).

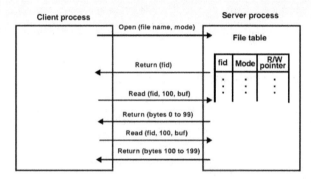

Fig. 3.3 An example of a stateful file server

To keep track of the current record position for each client that has opened the file for accessing. Therefore to design an idempotent interface for reading the next record from the file, it is important that each client keeps track of its own current record position and the server is made stateless, that is, no client state should be maintained on the server side. Based on this idea, an idempotent procedure for reading the next record from a sequential file is

ReadRecordN (Filename, N)

which returns the Nth record from the specified file. In this case, the client has to correctly specify the value of n to get desired record from the file.
However, not all non idempotent interfaces can be so easily transformed to an Idempotent form. For example, consider the following procedure for appending a new record to the same sequential file.

AppendRecord (Filename, Record)

It is clearly not idempotent since repeated execution will add further copies of the same record to the file. This interface may be converted into an idempotent interface by using the following two procedures instead of the one defined above :

41

GetLastRecordNo (Filename)
WriteRecordN (Filename, Record, N)

The first procedure returns the record number of the last record currently in the file, and the second procedure writes a record at specified in the file. Now, for appending a record, the client will have to use the following two procedures :

Last = GetLastRecordNo (Filename)
WriteRecordN (Filename, Record, Last)

For exactly-once semantics, the programmer is relieved of the burden of implementing the server procedure in an idempotent manner because the call semantics itself takes care of executing the procedure only once. The implementation of exactly-once call semantics is based on the use of timeouts, retransmissions, call identifiers with the same identifier for repeated calls, a reply cache associated with the callee.

4.1 COMMUNICATION PROTOCOLS FOR RPCS

Different systems, developed on the basis of remote procedure calls, have different IPC requirements. Based on the needs of different systems, several communication protocols have been proposed for use in RPCs. A brief description of these protocols is given below.

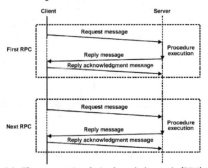

Fig. 4.1 : The request / reply / acknowledge reply (RRA)
protocol

In the RRA protocol, there is a   possibility that   the
acknowledgement message may itself get lost. Therefore implementation of the RRA protocol requires that the unique message identifiers associated with request messages must be ordered. Each reply message contains the message identifier of the corresponding request message, and each acknowledgement message also contains the name same message identifier. This helps in matching a reply with its corresponding request and an acknowledgement with its corresponding reply. A client acknowledges a reply message only if it has received the replies to all the requests previous to the request corresponding to this reply.

Thus an acknowledgement message is interpreted as acknowledging the receipt of all reply messages corresponding to the request messages with lower message identifiers. Therefore, the loss of an acknowledgement message is harmless.

4.2 COMPLICATED RPCs

The following are the two types of RPCs as complicated :

1. RPCs involving long-duration calls or large gaps between calls.
2. RPCs involving arguments and / or results that are too large to fit in a single datagram packet.

Different protocols are used for handling these two types of complicated RPCs.

4.3 CLIENT – SERVER BINDING

How does a client locate a server ?

1. Stubs are generated from a formal specification of a server's interface:

* procedure names, signatures, in/out, version, etc.

2. When server is initialized, it exports its interface by registering at a binder program with a handle (e.g., ip address and port)

3. Upon a remote-procedure call, if client not-bound yet, it imports interface from binder

4. Advantages:

location independence

can balance load

fault tolerance

authentication, version validation

5. Disadvantage:

costly (first lookup)

bottleneck, single-point of failure

It is necessary for a client to know the location of a server before a RPO call can take place between them. The process by which a client associated with a server so that calls can take place is known as binding. Here the server exports its operations to register its acceptance or availability to connect with the client. And client imports their operations.

4.4 EXCEPTION HANDLING

We saw in Figure 4.1 that when a remote procedure cannot be executed successfully, the server reports an error in the reply message. An RPC also fails when a client cannot contact the server of the RPC. An RPC system must have an effective exception – handling mechanism for reporting such failures to clients. One approach to do this is to define an exception condition for each possible error type and have the corresponding exception raised when an error of that type occurs, causing the exception-handling procedure to be called and automatically executed in the client's environment. This approach can be used with those programming languages that provide language constructs for exception handling. Some such programming languages are ADA, CLU, and Modula – 3. In C language, signal handlers can be used for the purpose of exception handling.

However, not every language has an exception – handling mechanism. For example, Pascal does not have such a mechanism. RPC systems designed for use with such languages generally use the method provided in conventional operating systems for exception handling. One such method is to return a well-known value to the process, making a system call to indicate failure and to report the type of error by storing a suitable value in a variable in the environment of the calling program. For example, in UNIX the value – 1 is used to indicate failure, and the type of error is reported in the global variable erino. In an RPC, a return value indicating an error is used both for errors due to failure to communicate with the server and errors reported in the reply message from the server. The details of the type of error is reported by storing a suitable value in a global variable in the client program. This approach suffers from two main drawbacks. First, it requires the client to test every return value. Second, it is not general enough because a return value used to indicate failure may be a perfectly legal value to be returned by a procedure. For example, if the value – 1 is used to indicate failure, this value is also the return value of a procedure call with arguments – 5 and 4 to a procedure for getting the sum of two numbers.

4.5 SECURITY

Some implementations of RPC include facilities for client and server authentication as well as for providing encryption – based security for calls. For example, callers are given a guarantee of the identity of the callee, and vice versa, by using the authentication service of Grapevine. For full end-to-end encryption of calls and results, the federal data encryption standard is used in. The encryption techniques provide protection from eavesdropping (and conceal pattern of data) and detect attempts at modification, replay, or creation of calls.

In other implementations of RPC that do not include security facilities, the arguments and results of RPC are readable by anyone monitoring communications between the caller and the callee. Therefore, in this case, if security is desired, the user must implement his or her own authentication and data encryption mechanisms.

When designing an application, the user should consider the following security issues related with the communication of messages :

> 1. Is the authentication of the server by the client required?
> 2. Is the authentication of the client by the server required when the result is returned?
> 3. Is it all right if the arguments and results of the RPC are accessible to users other than the caller and the callee?

4.6 SOME SPECIAL TYPES OF RPCs

4.6.1 Callback RPC :

In the usual RPC protocol, the caller and callee processes have a client – server relationship. Unlike this, the callback RPC facilitates a peer-to-peer paradigm among the participating processes. It allows a process to be both a client and a server.

Callback RPC facility is very useful in certain distributed applications. For example, remotely processed interactive applications that need user input from time to time or under special conditions for further processing require this type of facility. In such applications, the client process makes an RPC to the concerned server process, and during procedure execution for the client, the server process makes a callback RPC to the client process. The client process takes necessary action based on the server's request and returns a reply for the call back RPC to the server process. On receiving this reply, the server resumes the execution of the procedure and finally returns the result of the initial call to the client. Note that the server may make several callbacks to the client before returning the result of the initial call to the client process.

The ability for a server to call its client back is very important, and care is needed in the design of RPC protocols to ensure that it is possible. In particular, to provide callback RPC facility, the following are necessary :

> 1. Providing the server with the client's handle
> 2. Making the client process wait for the callback
> RPC
> 3. Handling callback deadlocks

4.6.2 Commonly used methods to handle these issues are described below.

Notation in one machine architecture and in 2's complement notation in another machine architecture. Floating-point representations may also vary between two different machine architectures. Therefore, an RPC system for a heterogeneous environment must be designed to take care of such differences in data representations between the architectures of client and server machines of a procedure call.

1. **Transport protocol :** For better portability of applications, an RPC system must be independent of the underlying network transport protocol. This will allow distributed applications using the RPC system to be run on different networks that use different transport protocols.

2. **Control protocol :** For better portability of applications, an RPC system must also be independent of the underlying network control protocol that defines control information in each transport packet to track the state of a call.

The most commonly used approach to deal with these types of heterogeneity while designing an RPC system for a heterogeneous environment is to delay the choices of data representation, transport protocol, and control protocol until bind time. In conventional RPC systems, all these decisions are made when the RPC system is designed. That is, the binding mechanism of an RPC system for a heterogeneous environment is considerably richer in information than the binding mechanism used by a conventional RPC system. It includes mechanisms for determining which data conversion software (if any conversion is needed), which transport protocol, and which control protocol should be used between a specific client and server and returns the correct procedures to the stubs as result parameters of the binding call. These binding mechanism details are transparent to the users. That is, application programs never directly access the component structures of the binding mechanism; they deal with bindings only as atomic types and acquire and discard them via the calls of the RPC system.

4.7 LIGHTWEIGHT RPC

The Lightweight Remote Procedure Call (LRPC) was introduced by Berhsad and integrated into the Taos operating system of the DEC SRC Firefly microprocessor workstation. The description below is based on the material in their paper.

Based on the size of the kernel, operating systems may be broadly classified into two categories – monolithic – kernel operating systems and microkernel operating systems. Monolithic – kernel operating systems have a large, monolithic kernel that is insulated from user programs by simple hardware boundaries. On the other hand, in microkernel operating systems, a small kernel provides only primitive operations and most of the services are provided by user-level servers. The servers are usually implemented as processes and can be programmed separately. Each server forms a component of the operating system and usually has its own address space. As compared to the monolithic – kernel approach, in this approach services are provided less efficiently because the various components of the operating system have to use some form of IPC to communicate with each other. The advantages of this approach include simplicity and flexibility. Due to modular structure, microkernel operating systems are simple and easy to design, implement, and maintain.

In the microkernel approach, when different components of the operating system have their own address spaces, the address space of each component is said to form a domain, and messages are used for all interdomain communication. In this case, the communication traffic in operating systems are of two types:

1. Cross-domain, which involves communication between domains on the same machine.
2. Cross-machine, which involves communication between domains located on separate machines.

The LRPC is a communication facility designed and optimized for cross-domain communications.

Although conventional RPC systems can be used for both cross-domain and cross machine communications. Bershad et al. observed that the use of conventional RPC systems for cross-domain communications, which dominate cross-machine communications, incurs an unnecessarily high cost. This cost leads system designers to coalesce weakly related components of microkernel operating systems into a single domain, trading safety and performance. Therefore, the basic advantages of using the microkernel approach are not fully exploited. Based on these observations, Bershad et al. designed the LRPC facility for cross-domain communications, which has better performance than conventional RPC systems. Nonetheless, LPRC is safe and transparent and represents a viable communication alternative for microkernel operating systems.

To achieve better performance than conventional RPC systems, the four techniques described below are used by LRPC.

4.7.1 Simple Control Transfer :

Whenever possible, LRPC uses a control transfer mechanism that is simpler than the used in conventional RPC systems. For example, it uses a special threads scheduling mechanism, called handoff scheduling for direct context switch from the client thread to the server thread of an LRPC. In this mechanism, when a client calls a server's procedure, it provides the server with an argument stack and its own thread of execution. The call causes a trap to the kernel. The kernel validates the caller, creates a call linkage, and dispatches the client's thread directly to the server domain, causing the server to start executing immediately. When the called procedure completes, control and results return through the kernel back to the point of the client's call. In contrast to this, is conventional RPC implementations, context switching between the client and server threads of an RPC is slow because the client thread and the server thread are fixed in their own domains, signaling one another at a rendezvous, and the critical domain transfer path. On the other hand, latency is reduced by reducing context switching overhead by caching domains on idle processors. This is basically a generalization of the idea of decreasing operating system latency by caching recently blocked threads on idle processors to reduce wake-up latency.

Instead of threads, LRPC caches domains so that any thread that needs to run in the context of an idle domain can do so quickly, not just the thread that ran there most recently.

It was found that LRPC achieves a factor-of-three performance improvement over more traditional approaches. Thus LRPC reduces the cost of cross-domain communication to nearly the lower bound imposed by conventional hardware.

4.8 OPTIMIZATIONS FOR BETTER PERFORMANCE

As with any software design, performance is an issue in the design of a distributed application. The description of LRPC shows some optimizations that may be adopted for better performance of distributed applications using RPC. Some other optimizations that may also have significant payoff when adopted for designing RPC based distributed applications are described below.

Concurrent Access to Multiple Servers :

Although one of the benefits of RPC is its synchronization property, many distributed applications can benefit from concurrent access to multiple servers. One of the following three approaches may be used for providing this facility :

1. The use of threads in the implementation of a client process where each thread can independently make remote procedure calls to different servers. This method requires that the addressing in the underlying protocol is rich enough to provide correct routing of responses.

2. Another method is the use of the early reply. As shown in Figure 3.5, in this method a call is split into two separate RPC calls, one passing the parameters to the server and the other requesting the result. In reply to the first call, the server returns a tag that is sent back with the second call to match the call with the correct result. The client decides the time delay between the two calls and carries out other activities during this period, possibly making several other RPC calls. A drawback of this method is that the server must hold the result of a call until the client makes a request for it. Therefore, if the request for results is delayed, it may cause congestion or unnecessary overhead at the server.

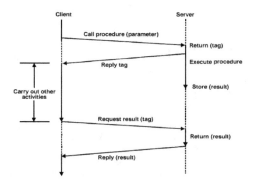

Fig. 4.2 : The early reply approach for providing the reality of concurrent access to multiple servers

3. The third approach, known as the call buffering approach, was proposed by Gimson [1985]. In this method, clients and servers do not interact directly with each other. They interact indirectly via a call buffer server. To make an RPC call, a client sends its call request to the call buffer server, where the request parameters together with the name of the server and the client are buffered. The client can then perform other activities until it needs the result of the RPC call. When the client reaches a state in which it needs the result, it periodically polls the call buffer server to see if the result of the call is available, and if so, it recovers the result. On the server side, when a server is free, it periodically polls the call buffer server to see if there is any call for it. If so, it recovers the call request, executes it, and makes a call back to the call buffer server to return the result of execution to the call buffer server. The method is illustrated in Figure 4.2

The Mercury communication system has a new data type called promise that is created during an RPC call and is given a type corresponding to those of the results and exceptions of the remote procedure. When the results arrive, they are stores in the appropriate promise from where the caller claims the results at a time suitable to it. Therefore, after making a call, a caller can continue with other work and subsequently pick up the results of the call from the appropriate promise.

A promise is in one of two states – blocked or ready. It is in a blocked state from the time of creation to the time the results of the call arrive, whereupon it enters the ready state. A promise in the ready state is immutable.

4

DISTRIBUTED SHARED MEMORY

5.1 CONSISTENCY MODELS

Consistency requirements vary from application to application. A consistency model basically refers to the degree of consistency that has to be maintained for the shared – memory data for the memory to work correctly for a certain set of applications. It is defined as a set of rules that applications must obey if they want to DSM system to provide the degree of consistency guaranteed by the consistency model. Several consistency models have been proposed in the literature. Of these, the main ones are described below.

It may be noted here that the investigation of new consistency models is currently an active area of research. The basic idea is to invent a consistency model that can allow consistency requirements to be related to a greater degree than existing consistency models, with the relaxation done in such a way that a set of applications can function correctly. This helps in improving the performance of these applications because better concurrency can be achieved by relaxing the consistency requirement. However, applications that depend on a stronger consistency model may not perform correctly if executed in a system that supports only a weaker consistency model. This is because if a system supports the stronger consistency model, then the weaker consistency model is automatically supported but the converse is not true.

5.2 STRICT CONSISTENCY MODEL

The strict consistency model is the strongest form of memory coherence, having the most stringent consistency requirement. A shared-memory system is said to support the strict consistency model if the value returned by a read operation on a memory address is always the same as the value written by the most recent write operation to that address, irrespective of the locations of the processes performing the read and write operations. That is, all writes instantaneously become visible to all processes.

Implementation of the strict consistency model requires the existence of an absolute global time so that memory read / write operations can be correctly ordered to make the meaning of "most recent" clear. However, absolute synchronization of clocks of all the nodes of a distributed system is not possible. Therefore, the existence of an absolute global time in a distributed system is also not possible. Consequently, implementation of the strict consistency model for a DSM system is practically impossible.

5.3 SEQUENTIAL CONSISTENCY MODEL

The sequential consistency model was proposed Lamport [1979]. A shared-memory system is said to support the sequential consistency model if all processes see the same order of all memory access operations on the shared memory. The exact order in which the memory access operations are interleaved does not matter.

That is, if the three operations read $r1$, write $w1$, read $r2$ are preformed on a memory address in that order, any of the orderings $(r1, w1, r2), (r1, r2, w1)$,$(w1, r1, r2), (w1, r2, r1), (r2, r1, w1), (r2, w1, r1)$ of the three operations is acceptable provided all processes see the same ordering. If one process sees one of the orderings of the three operations and another process sees a different one, the memory is not a sequentially consistent memory. Note here that the only acceptable ordering for a strictly consistent

memory is $r1$, $w1$, $r2$.

The consistency requirement of the sequential consistency model is weaker than that of the strict consistency model because the sequential consistency model does not guarantee that a read operation on a particular memory address always return the same value as written by the most recent write operation to that address. As a consequence, with a sequentially consistent memory, running a program twice may not give the same result in the absence of explicit synchronization operations. This problem does not exist in a strictly consistent memory.

A DSM system supporting the sequential consistency model can be implemented by ensuring that no memory operation is started until all the previous ones have been completed. A sequentially consistent memory provides one-copy / single-copy semantics because all the process sharing a memory location always see exactly the same contents stored in it. This is the most intuitively expected semantics for memory coherence. Therefore, sequential consistency is acceptable by most applications.

5.4 CAUSAL CONSISTENCY MODEL

The causal consistency model, relaxes the requirement of the sequential consistency model for better concurrency. Unlike the sequential consistency model, in the causal consistency model, all processes see only those memory reference operations in the same (correct) order that are potentially causally related. Memory reference operations that are not potentially causally related may be seen by different processes in different orders. A memory reference operation (Read / write) is said to be potentially causally related to another memory reference operation if the first one might have been influenced in any way by the second one. For example, if a process performs a read operation followed by a write operation, the write operation is potentially causally related to the read operation because the computation of the value written may have depended in some way on the value obtained by the read operation.

On the other hand, a write operation performed by one process is not causally related to a write operation performed by another process if the first process has not read either the value written by the second process or any memory variable that was directly or indirectly derived from the value written by the second process.

A shared memory system is said to support the causal consistency model if all write operations that are potentially causally related are seen by all processes in the same (correct) order. Write operations that are not potentially causally related may be seen by different processes in different orders. Note that "correct order" means that if a write operation w2 is causally related to another write operation w1 , the acceptable order is w1 , w2 because the value written by w2 might have been influenced in some way by the value written by w1 . Therefore, w2 , w1 is not an acceptable order.

5.5 REDUCTION

Shared variables that must be automatically modified may be annotated to be reduction type. For example, in a parallel computation application, a global minimum must be atomically fetched and modified if it is greater than the local minimum. In Munin, a reduction variable is always modified by being locked (acquire lock), read, updated, and unlocked (release lock). For better performance, a reduction variable is stored at a fixed owner that receives updates to the variable from other processes, synchronizes the updates received from different processes, performs the updates on the variable, and propagates the updated variable to its replica locations.

5.6 CONVENTIONAL

Shared variables that are not annotated as one of the above types are conventional variables. The already described release consistency protocol of Munin is used to maintain the consistency of replicated conventional variables. The write invalidation protocol is used in this case of ensure that no process ever reads a stale version of a conventional variable. The page containing a conventional variable is dynamically moved to the location of a process that wants to perform a write operation on the variable.

Experience with Munin has shown that read-only migratory, and write shared annotation types are very useful because variables of these types are frequently used, but producer, consumer, result and reduction annotation types are of little use because variable of these types are less frequently used.

5.7 REPLACEMENT STRATEGY

In DSM systems that allow shared memory blocks to be dynamically migrated / replicated, the following issues must be addressed when the available space for caching shared data fills up at a node :

1. Which block should be replaced to make space for a newly required block?
2. Where should the replaced block be placed?

5.8 WHICH BLOCK TO REPLACE

The problem of replacement has been studied extensively for paged main memories and shared memory multiprocessor systems. The usual classification of replacement algorithms group them into the following categories [Smith 1982] :

1. Usage based versus non-usage based : Usage based algorithms keep track of the history of usage of a cache line (or page) and use this information to make replacement decisions. That is, the reuse of a cache line normally improves the replacement status of that line. Least recently used (LRU) is an example of this type of algorithm. Conversely, non-usage-based algorithms do not take the record of use of cache lines into account when doing replacement. First in, first out (FIFO) and Rand (Random or pseudorandom) belong to this class.

2. Fixed space versus variable space : Fixed space algorithms assume that the cache size is fixed while variable space algorithms are based on the assumption that the cache size can be changed dynamically depending on the need. Therefore, replacement in fixed space algorithms simply involves the selection of a selection of a specific cache line. On the other hand, in a variable space algorithm, a fetch does not imply a replacement, and a swap out can take place without a corresponding fetch.

Variable space algorithms are not suitable for a DSM system became each node's memory that acts as cache for the virtually shared memory is fixed in size. Moreover, as compared to non usage based algorithms, usage based algorithms are more suitable for DSM systems because they allow to take advantage of the data access locality feature. However, unlike most caching systems, which use a simple LRU policy for replacement, most DSM systems differentiate the status of data items and use a priority spechanism. As an example, the replacement policy used by the DSM system of IVY [LL 1986, 1988] is presented here. In the DSM system of IVY, each memory block of a node is classified into one of the following five types.

1. Unused : A free memory block that is not currently being used.

2. Nil : A block that has been invalidated.

3. Read-only : A block for which the node has only read access right.

4. Read owned : A block for which the node has only read access right but is also the owner of the block.

5. Writable : A block for which the node has write access permission, Obviously, the node is the owner of the block because IVY uses the write invalidate protocol.

Based on this classification of blocks, the following replacement priority is used.

1. Both unused and nil blocks have the highest replacement priority. That is, they will be replaced first if a block is needed. It is obvious for an unused block to have the highest replacement priority. A nil block also has the same replacement priority because it is no longer useful and future access to the block would cause a network fault to occur. Notice that a nil block may be a recently referenced block, and this is exactly why a simple LRU policy is not adequate.

2. The read only blocks have the next replacement priority. This is because a copy of a read only block is available with its owner, and therefore it is possible to simply discard that block. When the node again requires that block in the future, the block has to be brought from its owner node at that time.

3. Read owned and writable blocks for which replica(s) exist on some other node(s) have the next replacement priority because it is sufficient to pass ownership to one of the replica nodes. The block itself need not be sent, resulting in a smaller message.

4. Read owned and writable blocks for which only this node has a copy have the lowest replacement priority because replacement of such a block involves transfer of the block's ownership as well as the block from the current node to some other nodes. An LRU policy is used to select a block for replacement when all the blocks in the local cache have the same priority.

5.9 WHERE TO PLACE A REPLACED BLOCK

Once a memory block has been selected for replacement, it should be ensured that if there is some useful information in the block, it should not be lost. For example, simply discarding a block having unused, Nil, or read only status does not lead to any loss of data. Similarly, discarding a read owned of a writable block for which replica(s) exist on some other node(s) is also harmless. However, discarding a read owned or a writable block for which there is no replica on any other node may lead to loss of useful data. Therefore, care must be taken to store them somewhere before discarding. The two commonly used approaches for storing a useful block at the time of its replacement are as follows :

1. **Using secondary store :** In this method, the block is simply transferred on to a local disk. The advantage of this method is that it does not waste any memory space and if the node wants to access the same block again, it can get the block locally without a need for network access.

2. Using the memory space of other nodes : Sometimes it may be faster to transfer a block over the network than to transfer it to a local disk. Therefore, another method for storing a useful block is to keep track of free memory space at all nodes in the system and to simply transfer the replaced block to the memory or a node with available space. This method requires each node to maintain a table of free memory space in all other nodes. This table may be updated by having each node piggyback its memory status information during normal traffic.

5.10 THRASHING

Thrashing is said to occur when the system spends a large amount of time transferring shared data blocks from one node to another, compared to the time spent doing the useful work of executing application processes. It is a serious performance problem with DSM systems that allow data blocks to migrate from one node to another. Thrashing may occur in the following situations :

1. When interleaved data accesses made by processes on two or more nodes causes a data block to move back and forth fro one node to another in quick succession (a ping – pong effect)

2. When blocks with read only permissions are repeatedly invalidated soon after they are replicated.

Such situations indicate poor (node) locality in references. If not properly handled, thrashing degrades system performance considerably. Therefore, steps must be taken to solve this problem. The following methods may be used to solve the thrashing problem in DSM systems :

1. Providing application – controlled locks : Locking data to prevent other nodes from accessing that for a short period of time can reduce thrashing. An application controlled lock can be associated with each data block to implement this method.

2. Nailing a block to a node for a minimum amount of time : Another method to reduce thrashing is to disallow a block to be taken away from a node until a minimum amount of time t elapses after its allocation to that node. The time t can either be fixed statically or be turned dynamically on the basis of access patterns. For example, Mirage [Fleisch and Popek 1989] employs this method to reduce thrashing and dynamically determines the minimum amount of time for which a block will be available at a node on the basis of access patterns.

The main drawback of this scheme is that it is very difficult to choose the appropriate value for the time. If the value is fixed statically, it is liable to be inappropriate in many cases. For example, if a process accesses a block for writing to it only once, other processes will be prevented from accessing the block until time t elapses. On the other hand, it a process accesses a block for performing several write operations on it, time t may elapse before the process has finished using the block and the system may grant permission to another process for accessing the block. Therefore, tuning the value of t dynamically is the preferred approach in this case, the value of t for a block can be decided based on past access patterns of the block. The MMU's reference bits may be used for this purpose. Another factor that may be used for deciding the value of t for a block is the length of a the queue of processes waiting for their turn to access the block.

3. Tailoring the coherence algorithm to the shared data usage pattern Thrashing can also minimized by using different coherence protocols for shared data having different characteristics. For example, the coherence protocol used in Munin for write shared variables avoids the false sharing problem, which ultimately results in the avoidance of thrashing.

Notice from the description above that complete transparency of distributed shared memory is compromised somewhat while trying to minimize thrashing. This is because most of the approaches described above require the programmer's assistance. For example, in the method of application controlled locks, the use of locks needs to be directed towards a particular shared memory algorithm and hence the shared memory
abstraction can no longer be transparent. Moreover, the application must be aware of the shared data it is accessing and its shared access patterns. Similarly, Munin requires programmers to annotate shared variables with standard annotation types, which makes the shared memory abstraction nontransparent.

2. **Smallest page size algorithm :** In this method, the DSM block size is taken as the smallest VM page size of all machines. If a page fault occurs on a node with a large page size, multiple blocks (whose total size is equal to the page size of the faulting node) are moved to satisfy the page fault. Although this algorithm reduces data contention, it suffers from the increased communication and block table management overheads associated with small sized blocks.

3. **Intermediate page size algorithm :** To balance between the problems of large and small sized blocks, a heterogeneous DSM system may select to choose a block size somewhere in between the largest VM page size and the smallest VM page size of all machines.

5.11 ADVANTAGES OF DSM

Distributed Shared Memory is a high level mechanism for interprocess communication in loosely coupled distributed systems. It is receiving increased attention because of the advantages it has over the message passing mechanisms. These advantages are discussed below.

5.12 SIMPLER ABSTRUCTION

By now it is widely recognized that directly programming loosely coupled distributed memory machines using message passing models is tedious and error phone. The main reason is that the message passing models force programmers to be conscious of data movement between processes at all times, since processes must explicitly use communication primitives and channels or ports. To alleviate this burden, RPC was introduced to provide a procedure call interface. However, even in RPC, since the procedure call is performed in an address space different from that of the caller's address space, it is difficult for the caller to pass context related data or complex data structures; that is, parameters must be passed by value. In the message passing model, the programming task is further complicated by the fact that data structures passed between processes in the front of messages must be packed and unpacked. The shared memory programming paradigm shields the application programmers from many such low level concerns. Therefore, the primary advantage of DSM is the simpler abstraction it provides to the application programmers of loosely coupled distributed memory machines.

5.13 BETTER PORTABILITY OF DISTRIBUTED APPLICATION PROGRAMS

The access protocol used in case of DSM is consistent with the way sequential applications access data. This allows for a more natural transition from sequential to distributed applications. In principle, distributed application programs written for a shared memory multiprocessor system can be executed on a distributed shared memory system without change. Therefore, it is easier to port an existing distributed application program to a distributed memory system with DSM facility than to a distributed men system without this facility.

5.14 BETTER PERFORMANCE OF SOME APPLICATIONS

The layer of software that provides DSM abstraction is implemented on top of a message passing system and uses the services of the underlying message passing communication system. Therefore, in principle, the performance of applications that the DSM is expected to be worse than if they use message passing directly. However, this is not always true, and it has been found that some applications using DSM can even outperform their message passing counterparts. This is possible for three reasons [Stumm and Zhou 1990] :

1. **Locality of data :** The communication model of DSM is to make the data more accessible by moving it around. DSM algorithms normally move data between nodes in large blocks. Therefore, in those applications that exhibit a reasonable degree of locality in their data accesses, communication overhead is amortized over multiple memory accesses. This ultimately results in reduced overall communication cost for such applications.

2. **On demand data movement :** The computation model of DSM also facilitates on demand movement of data as they are being accessed. On the other hand, there are several distributed applications that execute in phase, where each computation phase is preceded by a data exchange phase. The time needed for the data exchange phase is often dictated by the throughput of existing communication bottlenecks. Therefore, in such applications, the on demand data movement facility provided by DSM eliminates the data exchange phase, spreads the communication load over a longer period of time, and allows for a greater degree of concurrency.

3. **Larger memory space :** With DSM facility, the total memory size is the sum of the memory sizes of all the nodes in the system. Thus, paging and swapping activities, which involve disk access, are greatly reduced.

5.15 FLEXIBLE COMMUNICATION ENVIRONMENT

The message passing paradigm requires recipient identification and coexistence of the sender and receiver processes. That is, the sender process of a piece of data must know the names of its receiver processes (except in multicast communication), and the receivers of the data must exist at the time the data is sent and in a state that they can (or eventually can) receive the data. Otherwise, the data is undeliverable. In contrast, the shared memory paradigm of DSM provides a more flexible communication environment in which the sender process need not specify the identity of the receiver processes of the data. It simply places the data in the shared memory and the receivers access it directly from the shared memory. Therefore, the coexistence of the sender and receiver processes is also not necessary in the shared memory paradigm. In fact, the lifetime of the shared data is independent of the lifetime of any of its receiver processes.

5

SYNCHRONIZATION

Synchronization mechanisms that are suitable for distributed systems. In particular, the following synchronization related issues are described :

Clock synchronization
Event ordering
Mutual exclusion
Deadlock
Election algorithm

6.1 CLOCK SYNCHRONIZATION

Every computer needs a timer mechanism (called a computer clock) to keep track of current time and also for various accounting purposes such as calculating the time spent by a process in CPU utilization, disk I/O and so on, so that the corresponding user can be charged properly. In a distributed system, an application may have processes that concurrently run on multiple nodes of the system. For correct results, several such distributed applications require that the clocks of the nodes are synchronized with each other. For example, for a distributed on line reservation system to be fair, the only remaining seat booked almost simultaneously from two different nodes should be offered to the client who booked first, even if the time different between the two bookings is very small. It may not be possible to guarantee this if the clocks of the nodes of the system are not synchronized. In a distributed system, synchronized clocks also enable one to measure the duration of distributed activities that start on one node and terminate on another node, for instance calculating the time taken to transmit a message from one node to another at any arbitrary time. It is difficult to get the correct result in the case if the clocks of the sender and receiver nodes are not synchronized.

There are several other applications of synchronized clocks in distributed systems. Some good examples of such applications may be found in [Liskov 1993].

The discussion above shows that it is the job of a distributed operating system designer to devise and use suitable algorithms for properly synchronizing the clocks of a distributed system. This section presents a description of such algorithms. However, for a better understanding of these algorithms, we will first discuss how computer clocks are implemented and what are the main issues in synchronizing the clocks of a distributed system?

6.2 HOW COMPUTER CLOCKS ARE IMPLEMENTED

A computer clock usually consists of three components – a quartz crystal that oscillates at a well – defined frequency, a counter register, and a holding register. The holding register is used to store a constant value that is decided based on the frequency of oscillation of the quartz crystal. That is, the value in the counter register is decremented by 1 for each oscillation of the quartz crystal. When the value of the counter register becomes zero, an interrupt is generated and its value is reinitialized to the value in the holding register. Each interrupt is called clock tick. The value in the holding register is chosen 60 so that on 60 clock ticks occur in a second.

CMOS RAM is also present in most of the machines which keeps the clock of the machine up-to-date even when the machine is switched off. When we consider one machine and one clock, then slight delay in the clock ticks over the period of time does not matter, but when we consider n computers having n crystals, all running at a slightly different time, then the clocks get out of sync over the period of time. This difference in time values is called clock skew.

Tool Ordering of Events :

We have seen how a system of clocks satisfying the clock condition can be used to order the events of a system based on the happened before relationship among the events. We simply need to order the events by the times at which they occur. However that the happened before relation is only a partial ordering on the set of all events in the system. With this event ordering scheme, it is possible that two events *a* and *b* that are not related by the happened before relation (either directly or indirectly) may have the same timestamps associated with them.

6.3 MUTUAL EXCLUSION

There are several resources in a system that must not be used simultaneously by multiple processes if program operation is to be correct. For example, a file must not be simultaneously updated by multiple processes. Similarly, use of unit record peripherals such as tape drives or printers must be restricted to a single process at a time. Therefore, exclusive access to such a shared resource by a process must be ensured. This exclusiveness of access is called mutual exclusion between processes. The sections of a program that need exclusive access to shared resources are referred to as critical sections. For mutual exclusion, means are introduced to prevent processes from executing concurrently within their associated critical sections.

An algorithm for implementing mutual exclusion must satisfy the following requirements :

Issues in Recovery from Deadlock :

Two important issues in the recovery action are selection of victims and use of transaction mechanism. These are described below.

Selection of Victim(s): In any of the recovery approaches described above, deadlock is broken by killing or rolling back one or more processes. These processes are called victims. Notice that even in the operator intervention approach, recovery involves killing one or more victims. Therefore, an important issue in any recovery procedure is to select the victims. Selection of victim(s) is normally based on two major factors:

1. Minimization of recovery cost : This factor suggests that those processes should be selected as victims whose termination / rollback will incur the minimum recovery cost. Unfortunately, it is not possible to have a universal cost function, and therefore, each system should determine its own cost function to select victims. Some of the factors that may be considered for this purpose are (a) the priority of the processes;
(b) the nature of the processes, such as interactive or batch and possibility of return with no ill effects;
(c) the number and types of resources held by the processes;
(d) the length of service already received and the expected length of service further needed by the processes; and
(e) the total number of processes that will be affected.

2. Prevention of starvation : If a system only aims at minimization of recovery cost, it may happen that the same process (probably because its priority is very low) is repeatedly selected as a victim and may never complete. This situation known as starvation, must be somehow prevented in any practical system. One approach to handle this problem is to raise the priority of the process every time it is victimized. Another approach is to include the number of times a process is victimized as a parameter in the cost function.

Use of Transaction Mechanism: After a process is killed or rolled back for recovery from deadlock, it has to be return. However, rerunning a process may not always be safe, especially when the operations already performed by the process are non-idempotent. For example, if a process has updated the amount of a bank account by adding a certain amount to it, re-execution of the process will result in adding the same amount once again, leaving the balance in the account in an incorrect state. Therefore, the use of transaction mechanism (which ensures all or no effect) becomes almost inevitable for most processes when the system chooses the method of detection and recovery for handling deadlocks. However, notice that the transaction mechanism need not be used for those processes that can be rerun with no ill effects. For example, rerun of a compilation process has no ill effects because all it does is read a source file and produce an object file.

6.4 ELECTION ALGORITHMS

Several distributed algorithms require that there be a coordinator process in the entire system that performs some type of coordination activity needed for the smooth running of other processes in the system. Two examples of such coordinator processes encountered in this chapter are the coordinator in the centralized algorithm for mutual exclusion and the central coordinator in the centralized deadlock detection algorithm.

Since all other processes in the system have to interact with the coordinator, they all must unanimously agree on who the coordinator is. Furthermore, if the coordinator process fails due to the failure of the site on which it is located, a new coordinator process must be elected to take up the of the failed coordinator.

Election algorithms are meant for electing to take coordinator process from among the currently running processes in such a manner that at any instance of time there is a single coordinator for all processes in the system.

Election algorithm are based on the following assumptions :

> 1. Each process in the system has a unique priority number.
>
> 2. Whenever an election is held, the process having the highest priority number among the currently active processes is elected as the coordinator.
>
> 3. On recovery, a failed process can take appropriate actions to rejoin the set of active processes.

Therefore, whenever initiated, an election algorithm basically finds out which of the currently active processes has the highest priority number and then informs this to all other active processes. Different election algorithms differ in the way they do this. Two such election algorithms are described below.

6.4.1 Bully Algorithm:

When any process notices that the coordinator is no longer responding to the requests, it asks for the election.
Example: A process P holds an election as follows

> 1) P sends an ELECTION message to all the processes with higher numbers.
> 2) If no one responds, P wins the election and becomes the coordinator.
> 3) If one higher process answers; it takes over the job and P's job is done.

At any moment an "election" message can arrive to process from one of its lowered numbered colleague. The receiving process replies with an OK to say that it is alive and can take over as a coordinator. Now this receiver holds an election and in the end all the processes give uo except one and that one is the new coordinator.

The new coordinator announces its new post by sending all the processes a message that it is starting immediately and is the new coordinator of the system.

If the old coordinator was down and if it gets up again; it holds for an election which works in the above mentioned fashion. The biggest numbered process always wins and hence the name "bully" is used for this algorithm.

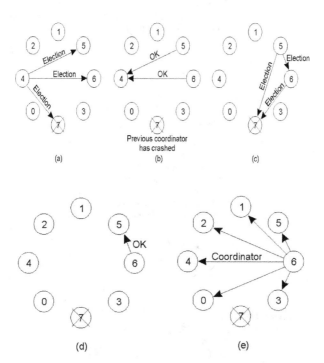

Figure 6.1: The bully election algorithm
Process 4 holds an election.
Process 5 and 6 respond, telling 4 to stop.
Now 5 and 6 each hold an election.
Process 6 tells 5 to stop.
Process 6 wins and tells everyone.

6.4.2 Ring Algorithm:

It is based on the use of a ring as the name suggests. But this does not use a toke. Processes are physically ordered in such a way that every process knows its successor.

When any process notices that the coordinator is no longer functioning, it builds up an ELECTION message containing its own number and passes it along the to its successor. If the successor is down, then sender skips that member along the ring to the next working process.

At each step, the sender adds its own process number to the list in the message effectively making itself a candidate to be elected s the coordinator. At the end, the message gets back to the process that started it.

That process identifies this event when it receives an incoming message containing its own process number. Then the same message is changed as coordinator and is circulated once again.

Example: two process, Number 2 and Number 5 discover together that the previous coordinator; Number 7 has crashed. Number 2 and Number 5 will each build an election message and start circulating it along the ring. Both the messages in the end will go to Number 2 and Number 5 and they will convert the message into the coordinator with exactly the same number of members and in the same order. When both such messages have gone around the ring, they both will be discarded and the process of election will re-start.

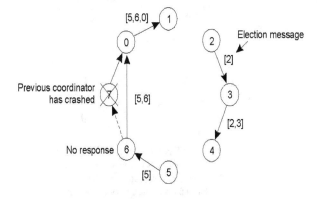

Figure6.2: Election algorithm using Ring

6.5 MUTUAL EXCLUSION

Mutual exclusion (often abbreviated to mutex) algorithms are used in concurrent programming to avoid the simultaneous use of a common resource, such as a global variable, by pieces of computer code called critical sections. A critical section is a piece of code in which a process or thread accesses a common resource. The critical section by itself is not a mechanism or algorithm for mutual exclusion. A program, process, or thread can have the critical section in it without any mechanism or algorithm which implements mutual exclusion.

Examples of such resources are fine-grained flags, counters or queues, used to communicate between code that runs concurrently, such as an application and its interrupt handlers. The synchronization of access to those resources is an acute problem because a thread can be stopped or started at any time. A mutex is also a common name for a program object that negotiates mutual exclusion among threads, also called a lock.

Following are the algorithms for mutual exclusion:

6.5.1 Centralized Algorithm

Here one process is selected as the coordinator of the system with the authority of giving access to other process for entering the critical region. If any process wants to enter the critical, it has to take the permission from the coordinator process. This permission is taking by sending a REQUEST message.

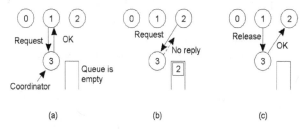

(a)   (b)   (c)

Figure: 6.3:
> Process 1 asks the coordinator for permission to enter a critical region. Permission is granted.
> Process 2 then asks permission to enter the same critical region. The coordinator does not reply.
> When process 1 exits the critical region, it tells the coordinator, when then replies to process 2.

65

As shown in figure 5.3-a), the coordinator is not reply to process 2 when the critical region is occupied. Here, depending on the type of system, the coordinator can also reply back to the process 2 that it is in queue. If the coordinator doesn't do so, then the waiting process 2 will be unable to distinguish between 'permission denied" or a "dead" coordinator.

This type of system as a single point of failure, if the coordinator fails, then the entire system crashes.

6.5.2 Distributed Algorithm:

A distributed algorithm for mutual exclusion is presented. No particular assumptions on the network topology are required, except connectivity; the communication graph may be arbitrary. The processes communicate by using messages only and there is no global controller. Furthermore, no process needs to know or learn the global network topology. In that sense, the algorithm is more general than the mutual exclusion algorithms which make use of an a priori knowledge of the network topology.

When a process wants to enter a critical region, it builds a message containing:

> 1. name of the critical region
> 2. it's process number
> 3. it's current time.

The process sends this message to all the processes in the network. When another process receives this message, it takes the action pertaining on its state and the critical region mentioned. Three cases are possible here:

> 1. If the message receiving process is not in the critical region and does not wish to enter it, it sends it back.
> 2. Receiver is already in the critical region and does not reply
> 3. Receiver wants to enter the same critical region and a
> 4. Has not done so, it compares the "time stamp" of the incoming message with the one it has sent to others for permission. The lowest one wins and can enter the critical region.

When the process exists from the critical region, it sends an OK message to inform everyone.

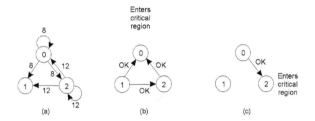

Figure 6.4:
a) Two processes want to enter the same critical region at the same moment.
b) Process 0 has the lowest timestamp, so it wins.
c) When process 0 is done, it sends an OK also, so 2 can now enter the critical region.

Disadvantage:

1. If one process crashes, it will fail to respond. Thus other possesses will assume that the process is still working in the critical region which will make other processes go through a starvation.

2. Here each process must maintain the group membership list that includes processes entering or leaving the group.

3. Here all the processes are involved in all decisions; this could lead to bottle neck when the numbers of processes in the group are more.

4. This algorithm is comparatively expensive, slower and complex.

6.5.3 Token Ring Algorithm:

Here we have a bus network (e.g., Ethernet), with no inherent ordering of the processes. In software, a logical ring is constructed in which each process is assigned a position in the ring. The ring positions may be allocated in numerical order of network addresses or some other means. It does not matter what the ordering is. All that matters is that each process knows who is next in line after itself.

When the ring is initialized, process 0 is given a token. The token circulates around the ring. It is passed from process k to process k +1 in point-to-point messages. When a process acquires the token from its neighbour, it checks to see if it is attempting to enter a critical region. If so, the process enters the region, does all the work it needs to, and leaves the region. After it has exited, it passes the token along the ring. It is not permitted to enter a second critical region using the same token. If a process is handed the token by its neighbour and is not interested in entering a critical region, it just passes it along. As a consequence, when no processes want to enter any critical regions, the token just circulates at high speed around the ring.

The correctness of this algorithm is easy to see. Only one process has the token at any instant, so only one process can actually be in a critical region. Since the token circulates among the processes in a well-defined order, starvation cannot occur. Once a process decides it wants to enter a critical region, at worst it will have to wait for every other process to enter and leave one critical region.

As usual, this algorithm has problems too. If the token is ever lost, it must be regenerated. In fact, detecting that it is lost is difficult, since the amount of time between successive appearances of the token on the network is unbounded. The fact that the token has not been spotted for an hour does not mean that it has been lost; somebody may still be using it.

The algorithm also runs into trouble if a process crashes, but recovery is easier than in the other cases. If we require a process receiving the token to acknowledge receipt, a dead process will be detected when its neighbour tries to give it the token and fails. At that point the dead process can be removed from the group, and the token holder can throw the token over the head of the dead process to the next member down the line, or the one after that, if necessary. Of course, doing so requires that everyone maintains the current ring configuration.

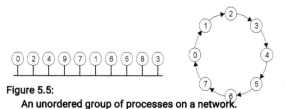

Figure 5.5:
An unordered group of processes on a network.
A logical ring constructed in software. (b)

6

RESOURCE MANAGEMENT- I

7.1 DESIRABLE FEATURES OF A GOOD GLOBAL SCHEDULES ALGORITHM

7.1.1 No A Priori knowledge about the Processes:

A good process scheduling algorithm should operate with absolutely no a priori knowledge about the processes to be executed. Scheduling algorithms that operate based on the information about the characteristics and resource requirements of the processes normally pose an extra burden upon the users who must specify this information while submitting their processes for execution.

7.1.2 Dynamic in Nature :

It is intended that a good process scheduling algorithm should be able to take care of the dynamically changing load (or status) of the various nodes of the system. That is, process assignment decisions should be based on the current load of the system and not on some fixed static policy. For this, sometimes it is also recommended that the scheduling algorithm should possess the flexibility to migrate a process more than once because the initial decision of placing a process on a particular node may have to be changed after some time to adapt to the new system load. This feature may also require that the system support preemptive process migration facility in which a process can be migrated from one node to another during the course of its execution.

7.1.3 Quick Decision Making Capability :

A good process scheduling algorithm must make quick decisions about the assignment of processes to processors. This is an extremely important aspect of the algorithms and makes many potential solutions unsuitable. For example, an algorithm that models the system by a mathematical program and solves it on line is unsuitable because it does not meet this requirement. Heuristic methods requiring less computational effort while providing near optimal results are therefore normally preferable to exhaustive (optimal) solution methods.

7.1.4 Balanced System Performance and Scheduling Overhead

Several global scheduling algorithms collect global state information and use this information in making process assignment decisions. A common intuition is that greater amounts of information describing global system state allow more intelligent process assignment decisions to be made that have a positive affect on the system as a whole. In a distributed environment, however, information regarding the state of the system is typically gathered at a higher cost than in a centralized system. The general observation is that, as overhead is increased in an attempt to obtain more information regarding the global state of the system, the usefulness of that information is decreased due to both the aging of the information being gathered and the low scheduling frequency as a result of the cost of gathering and processing that information. Hence algorithms that provide near optimal system performance with a minimum of global state information gathering overhead are desirable.

7.1.5 Stability :

A scheduling algorithm is said to be unstable if it can enter a state in which all the nodes of the system are spending all of their time migrating processes without accomplishing any useful work in an attempt to properly schedule the processes for better performance. This form of fruitless migration of processes is known as processor thrashing. Processor thrashing can occur in situations where each node of the system has the power of scheduling its own processes and scheduling decisions either are made independently of decisions made by other processors or are based on relatively old data de to transmission delay between nodes. For example, it may happen that node n1 and n2 both observe that node n3 is idle and then both offload a portion of their work to node n3 without being aware of the offloading decision made by the other. Now if node n3 becomes overloaded due to the processes received from both nodes n1 and n2 , then it may again start transferring its processes to other nodes. This entire cycle may be repeated again and again, resulting in an unstable state. This is certainly not desirable for a good scheduling algorithm.

7.2 TASK ASSIGNMENT APPROACH

7.2.1 The Basic Idea:

In this approach, a process is considered to be composed of multiple tasks and the goal is to find an optimal assignment policy for the tasks of an individual process. Typical assumptions found in task assignment work are as follows :

> A process has already been split into pieces called tasks. This split occurs along natural boundaries, so that each task will have integrity in itself and data transfers among the tasks will be minimized.

> The amount of computation required by each task and the speed of each processor are known.

The cost of processing each task on every node of the system is known. This cost is usually derived based on the information about the speed of each processor and the amount of computation required by each task.

The Interprocesses Communication (IPC) costs between every pair of tasks is known. The IPC cost of considered zero (negligible) for tasks assigned to the same node. They are usually estimated by an analysis of the static program of a process. For example during the execution of the process, if two tasks communicate n times and average time for each intertask communication is t, the intertask communication cost for the two tasks is $n\,t$.

Other constraints, such as resource requirements of the tasks and the available resources at each node, precedence relationships among the tasks, and so on, are also known.

Reassignment of the tasks is generally not possible.

With these assumptions, the task assignment algorithms seek to assign the tasks of a process to the nodes of the distributed system in such a manner so as to achieve goals such as the following.

1. Minimization of IPC costs
2. Quick turnaround time for the complete process
3. A high degree of parallelism
4. Efficient utilization of system resources in general

7.3 PROCESS MIGRATION

Process migration is the relocation of a process from its current location (the source node) to another node (the destination node). The flow of execution of a migrating process is illustrated in Figure 7.1.

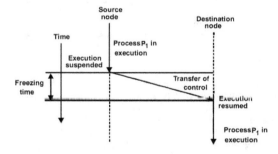

Fig 7.1 : Flow of execution of a migrating process

A process may be migrated either before it starts executing on its source node on during the course of its execution. The former is known as non-preemptive process migration, and the latter is known as preemptive process migration. Preemptive process migration is costlier than non-preemptive process migration since the process environment must also accompany the process to its new node for an already executing process.

Process migration involves the following major steps :

1. Selection of a process that should be migrated.
2. Selection of the destination node to which the selected process should be migrated
3. Actual transfer of the selected process to the destination node.

The first two steps are taken care of by the process migration policy and the third step is taken care of by the process migration mechanism. The policies for the selection of a source node, a destination node, and the process to be migrated on resource management.

7.4 DESIRABLE FEATURES OF A GOOD PROCESS MIGRATION

A good migration mechanism must process transparency, minimal interferences, minimal residue dependencies, efficiency, robustness, and communication between co-processes.

7.4.1 Transparency:

Transparency is an important requirement for a system that supports process migration. The following levels of transparency can be identified :

1. Object access level : Transparency at the object access level is the minimum requirement for a system to support non – preemptive process migration facility. If a system supports transparency at the object access level, access to objects such as files and devices can be done in a location independent manner. Thus, the object access level transparency allows free initiation of programs at an arbitrary node. Of course, to support transparency at object access level, the system must provide a mechanism for transparent object naming and locating.

System cal and interprocess communication level. So that a migrated process does not continue to depend upon its originating node after being migrated. It is necessary that all system calls, including interprocess communication, are location independent. Thus, transparency at this level must be provided in a system that is to support preemptive process migration facility. However, system calls to request the physical properties of a node need not be location independent.

Transparency of interprocess communication is also the transparent redirection of messages during the transient state of process that recently migrated. That is, once a message sent, it should reach its receiver process without the need for resending a from the sender node is sure the receiver process moves to another node before the message is received.

7.4.2 Minimal Interference :

Migration of a process should cause minimal interference to the progress of the process involved the system as a whole. One method to achieve this is by minimizing the freezing time of the process being migrated. Freezing time is defined as the time period for which the execution of the process is stopped for transferring its information to the destination node.

7.4.3 Minimal Residual Dependencies:

No residual dependency should be left on the previous node. That is, a migrated process should not in any way continue to depend on its previous node once it has started executing on its new node since, otherwise, the following will occur.

It may be noted that in the model described above, the tasks of a process were assigned to the various nodes of the system. This model may be generalized to the general task assignment problem in which several processes are to be assigned. In this case, each process is treated to be a task of the process force and the inter-process communication costs are assumed to be known.

Several extensions to the basic task assignment model described above have been proposed in the literature. In addition to the task assignment cost and the inter-task communication cost parameters of the basic task assignment model, the extended models take into account to her parameters such as memory size requirements of the task and memory size constraint of the processors, precedence relationship among the tasks, and so on. However, we will not discuss this topic any further because of the limited applicability of the task assignment approach in practical situations.

7.4.4 Load Balancing Approach :

The scheduling algorithms using this approach are known as load balancing algorithms or load leveling algorithms. These algorithms are based on the intuition that, for better resource utilization. It is desirable for the load in a distributed system to be balanced evenly. Thus, a load balancing algorithm tries to balance the total system load by transparently transferring the workload from heavily loaded nodes to lightly nodes in an attempt to ensure good overall performance relative to some specific metric of system performance. When considering performance from the user point of view, the metric involved is often the response time of the processes. However, when performance is considered from the resources point of view, the metric involved is the total systems throughput.

In contrast to response time, throughput is concerned with seeing that all users are treated fairly and that all are making progress. Notice that the resource view of maximizing resource utilization is compatible with the desire to maximize system throughput. Thus the basic goal of almost all the load balancing algorithms is to maximize the total system throughput.

7.4.5 Taxonomy of Load Balancing Algorithms :

The taxonomy presented here is a hierarchy of the features of load balancing algorithms. The structure of the taxonomy is shown in Figure. To describe a specific load balancing algorithm, a taxonomy user traces paths through the hierarchy. A description of this taxonomy is given below.

7.4.6 Static Versus Dynamic :

At the highest level, we may distinguish between static and dynamic load balancing algorithms. Static algorithms use only information about the average behaviour of the system, ignoring the current state of the system. On the other hand, dynamic algorithms react to the system state that changes dynamically.

7.4.7 Migration Limiting Policies :

Another important policy to be used by a distributed operating system that supports process migration is to decide about the total number of times a process should be allowed to migrate. One of the following two policies may be used for this purpose.

> **Uncontrolled :** In this case, remote process arriving at a node is treated just as a process originating at the node. Therefore, under this policy, a process may be migrated any number of times. This policy has the unfortunate property of causing instability.

> **Controlled :** To overcome the instability problem of the uncontrolled policy, most systems treat remote processes different from local processes and use a migration count parameter to fix a limit on the number of times that a process may migrate. Several system designers feel that process migration is an expensive operation and hence a process should not be allowed to migrate too frequently. Hence this group of designers normally favors an irrevocable migration policy. That is, the upper limit of the value of migration count is fixed to t, and hence a process cannot be migrated more than once under this policy. However, some system designers feel that multiple process migrations, especially for long processes, may be very useful for adapting to the dynamically changing states of the nodes. Thus this group of designers sets the upper limit of the value of migration count to some value k 1 . The value of k may be decided either statically of dynamically.

Its value may also be different for processes having different characteristics. For example, a long process (a process whose execution time is large) may be allowed to migrate more times as compared to a short process.

7.5 LOAD SHARING APPROACH

Several researchers believe that load balancing with its implication of attempting to equalize workload on all the nodes o the system, is not an appropriate objective. This is because the overhead involved in gathering state information to achieve this objective is normally very large, especially in distributed systems having a large number of nodes. Moreover, load balancing in the sense is not achievable because the number of processes in a node is always fluctuating and the temporal unbalance among the nodes exists at every moment, even if the static (average) load is perfectly balanced for the proper utilization the resources of a distributed system, it is not required to balance the load on all the nodes. Rather, it is necessary and sufficient to prevent the nodes from being idle while some other nodes have more than two processes. Therefore this rectification is often called dynamic load sharing instead of dynamic load balancing.

7.5.1 Issues in Designing Load Sharing Algorithms :

Similar to the load balancing algorithms, the design of a load sharing algorithm also requires that proper decisions be made regarding load estimation policy, process transfer policy, state information exchange policy, location policy, priority assignment policy, and with threads facility, a process having a single thread corresponds to a process of a traditional operating system. Threads are often referred to as lightweight processes and traditional processes are referred to as heavyweight processes.

7.5.2 Motivations for Using Threads :

The main motivations for using a multithreaded process instead of multiple single threaded processes for performing some computation activities are as follows :

1. The overheads involved in creating a new process are in general considerably greater than those of creating a new thread within a process.

2. Switching between threads sharing the same address space is considerably cheaper than switching between processes that have their own address space.

3. Threads allow parallelism to be combined with sequential execution and blocking system calls. Parallelism improves performance and blocking system calls make programming easier make programming easier.

4. Resource sharing can be achieved more efficiently and naturally between threads of a process than between processes because all threads of a process share the same address space.

These advantages are elaborated below:

The overheads involved in the creation of a new process and building its execution environment are liable to be much greater than creating a new thread within an existing process. This is mainly because when a new process is created its address space has to be created from scratch, although a part of it might be inherited from the process's parent process. However, when a new thread is created, it uses the address space of its process that need not be created from scratch. For instance, in case of a kernel supported virtual memory system, a newly created process will incur page faults as date and instructions are referenced for the first time. Moreover, hardware caches will initially contain no data values for the new process, and cache entries for the process's data will be created as the process executes. These overheads may also occur in thread creation, but they are liable to be less. This is because when the newly created thread accesses code and data that have recently been accessed by other threads within the process, it automatically takes advantage of any hardware or main memory caching that has taken place.

Threads also minimize context switching time, allowing the CPU to switch from one unit of computation to another unit of computation with minimal overhead. Due to the sharing of address space and other operating system resources among the threads of a process, the overhead involved in CPU switching among peer threads is very small as compared to CPU switching among processes having their own address spaces. This is the reason why threads are called lightweight processes.

> **True file service:** It is concerned with the operation on individual files, such operations for accessing and modifying the data in files and for creating and deleting. To perform these primitive file operations correctly and efficiently, typical design issues of a true file service component include file accessing mechanism, file sharing semantics, file caching mechanism, file replication mechanism, concurrency control mechanism, data consistency and multiple copy update protocol, and access control mechanism. Note that the separation of the storage service from the true file service makes it easy to combine different methods of storage and different storage media in a single file system.

> **Name service :** IT provides a mapping between text names for files and references to files, that is, file IDs. Text names are required because, file IDs are awkward and difficult for human users to remember and use. Most file systems use directories to perform this mapping. Therefore, the name service is also known as a directory service.

The directory service is responsible for performing directory related activities such as creation and deletion of directories, adding a new file to a directory deleting a file from a directory, changing the name of a file, moving a file from one directory to another, and so on.

The design and implementation of the storage service of a distributed file system is similar to that of the storage service of a centralized file system. Readers interested in the details of the storage service may refer to any good book on operating systems. Therefore, this chapter will mainly deal with the design and implementation issues of the true file service component of distributed file systems.

7

RESOURCE MANAGEMENT - II

7.1 FEATURES OF A GOOD DISTRIBUTED FILE SYSTEM

A good distributed file system should have the features described below.

1.Transparency : The following four types of transparencies are desirable :

Structure transparency : Although not necessary, for performance, scalability and reliability reasons, a distributed file system normally uses multiple file servers. Each file server is normally a user process or sometimes a kernel process that is responsible for controlling a set of secondary storage device (used for file storage) of the node on which it runs. In multiple file servers, the multiplicity of file servers should be transparent to the clients of a distributed file system. In particular, clients should not know the number or locations of the file servers and the storage devices. Ideally, a distributed file system should look to its clients like a conventional file system offered by a centralized, time-sharing operating system.

7.2 FILE MODELS

Different file systems use different conceptual models of a file. The two most commonly used criteria for file modeling are structure and modifiability. File models based on these criteria are described below :

7.2.1 Unstructured and Structured Files :

According to the simplest model, a file is an unstructured sequence of data. In this model, there is no substructure known to the of each file of the file system appears to the file server as an uninterrupted sequence of bytes. The operating system is not interested in the information stored in the files, the interpretation of the meaning and structure of the data stored in the files are entirely up to the application programs. UNIX and MS-DOS use this fie model.

Another file model that is rarely used nowadays is the structured file model. In this model, a file appears to the file server as an ordered sequence of records. Records of different files of the same file system can be of different size. Therefore, many types of files exist in a file system, each having different properties. In this model a record is the smallest unit of file data that can be accessed, and the files system read or write operations are carried out on a set of records.

Structured files are again of two types – files with non-indexed records and files with indexed records. In the former model, a file record is accessed by specifying its position within the file, for example, the fifth record from the beginning of the file or the second record from the end of the file. In the latter model, records have one or more key fields and can be addressed by specifying the values of the key fields. In file systems that allow indexed records, a file is maintained as a B-tree or other suitable data structure or a hash able is used to locate records quickly.

Most modern operating systems use the unstructured file model. This is mainly because sharing of a file by different applications is easier with the unstructured file model as compared to the structured file model. Since a file has no structure in the unstructured model, different applications can interpret the contents of a file m different ways.

In addition to data items, files also normally have attributes. A file's attributes are information describing that file. Each attribute has a name and a value. For example, typical attributes of a file may contain information such as owner, size, access permissions, date of creation, date of last modification, and date of last access. Users can read and update some of the attribute values using the primitives provided by the file system. Notice, however, that although a user may update the value of any attribute, not all attributes are user modifiable. For example, a user may update the value of the access permission attribute, but he or she cannot change the value of the size or date of creation attributes. The types of attributes that can be associated with a file are normally fixed by the file system. However, a file system may be designed to provide the flexibility to create and manipulate user defined attributes in addition to those supported by the file system.

File attributes are normally maintained and used by the directory service because they are subject to different access controls than the file they describe. Notice that although file attributes are maintained and used by the directory service, they are store with the corresponding file rather than with the file name in the directory. This is mainly because many directory systems allow files to be referenced by more than one name.

7.2.2 Mutable and Immutable Files :

According to the modifiability criteria, files are of two types – mutable and immutable. Most existing operating systems use the mutable file model. In this model, an update performed on a file overwrites on its old contents to produce the new contents That is, a file is represented as a single stored sequence that is altered by each update operation.

On the other hand, some more recent file systems, such as the Cedar File System (CFS), use the immutable file model. In this model, a file cannot be modified once it has been created except to be deleted. The file versioning approach is normally used to implement file updates, and each file is represented by a history of immutable versions.

That is, rather than updating the same file, a new version of the file is created each time a change is made to the file contents and the old version is retained unchanged. In practice, the use of storage space may be reduced by keeping only a record of the differences between the old and new versions rather than creating the entire file once again.

Gifford et al. emphasized that sharing only immutable files makes it easy to support consistent sharing. Due to this feature, it is much easier to support file caching and replication in a distributed system with the immutable file model because it eliminates all the problems associated with keeping multiple copies of a file consistent. However, due to the need to keep multiple versions of a file, the immutable file mode, suffers from two potential problems – increased use of disk space and increased disk allocation activity. Some mechanism is normally used to prevent the desk space from filling instantaneously.

7.3 FILE ACCESSING MODELS

The manner in which a client's request to access a file is serviced depends on the file accessing model used by the file system. The file accessing model of a distributed file system mainly depends on two factors – the method used for accessing remote files and the unit of data access.

Byte level transfer model : In this model, file data transfers across the network between a client and a server take place in units of bytes. This model provides maximum flexibility because it allows storage and retrieval of an arbitrary sequential subrange of a file, specified by an offset within a file, and a length. The main drawback of this model is the difficulty in cache management due to the variable length data for different access requests. The Cambridge File Server [Dion 1980, Mitchell and Dion 1982, Needham and Herbert 1982] uses this model.

Record level transfer mode : The three file data transfer models described above are commonly used with unstructured file models. The record level transfer model is suitable for use with those file models in which file contents are structured in the form of records. In this model, file data transfers across the network between a client and a server take place in units of records. The Research Storage System (RSS) [Gray 1978 Gray et al. 1981], which supports complex access methods to structured and indexed files, uses the record level transfer mode.

7.4 FILE SHARING SEMANTICS

A shared file may be simultaneously accessed by multiple users. In such a situation, an important design issue for any file system is to clearly defined when modifications of file data made by a user are observable by other users. This is defined by the type of file sharing semantics adopted by a file system.

1. UNIX semantics : this semantics enforces an absolute time ordering on all operations and ensures that every read operation on a file sees the effects of all previous write operations performed on that file **[Fig. 8.1(a)]**. In particular, writes to an open file by a user immediately become visible to other users who have this file open at the same time.

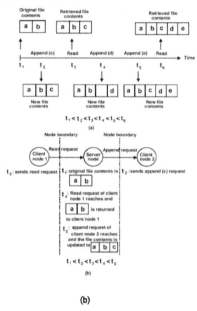

(b)

Fig. 8.1 : (a) Example of UNIX file sharing semantics; (b) an example explaining why it is difficult to achieve UNIX semantics in a distributed file system even what the shared file is handled by a single server

The UNIX semantics is commonly implemented in file systems for single processor systems because it is the most desirable semantics and also because it is easy to serialize all read/write requests. However, implementing UNIX semantics in a distributed file system is not an easy task. One may think that this semantics can be achieved in a distributed system by disallowing files to be cached at client nodes and allowing a shared file to be manage by only one file server that processes all read and write requests for the file strictly in the order in which it receives them. However, even with this approach, there is a possibility that, due to network delays, client requests from different nodes may arrive and get processed at the server node in an order different from the actual order in which the requests were made.

Furthermore, having all fie access requests processed by a single server and disallowing caching on a client nodes is not desirable in practice due to poor performance, poor scalability, and poor reliability of the distributed file system. Therefore, distributed file systems normally implement a more relaxed semantics of file sharing. Applications that need to guarantee UNIX semantics for correct functioning should use special means (e.g. locks) for this purpose and should not rely on the underlying semantics of sharing provided by the file system.

8

DISTRIBUTED FILE SYSTEM

8.1 FILE CACHING SCHEME

File caching has been implemented in several file systems for centralized time sharing systems to improve file I/O performance. The idea in file caching in these systems is to retain recently accessed file data in main memory, so that repeated accesses to the same information can be handled without additional disk transfers. Because of locality in file access patterns, file caching reduces disk transfers substantially, resulting in better overall performance of the file systems. The property of locality in file access patterns can as well be exploited in distributed systems by designing a suitable file caching scheme. In addition to better performance, a file caching scheme for a distributed file system may also contribute to its scalability and reliability because it is possible to cache remotely located data on a client node. Therefore, every distributed file system in serious use today uses some form of file caching. Even AT & T's Remote File System (RFS) which initially avoided caching to emulate UNIX semantics, now uses it.

In implementing a file caching scheme for a centralized file system one has to make several key decisions, such as the granularity of cached data (large versus small), cache size (large versus small, fixed versus dynamically changes, and the replacement policy. A good summary of these design issues is presented in [Smith 1+82]. In addition to these issues, a file caching scheme for a distributed file system should also address the following key decisions :

1. Cache location
2. Modification propagation
3. Cache validation

These three design issues are described below.

8.1.1 Cache Location :

Cache location refers to the place where the cached data is stored. Assuming that the original location of a file is on its server's disk, there are three possible cache locations in a distributed file system.

In this approach, a read quorum of r votes is collected to read a file and a write quorum of w votes to write a file. Since the votes assigned to each copy are not the same, the size of a read / write quorum depends on the copies selected for the quorum. The number of copies in the quorum will be less if the number of votes assigned to the selected copies is relatively more.

On the other hand, the number of copies in the quorum will be more if the number of votes assigned to the selected copies is relatively less. Therefore, to guarantee that there is a non-null intersection between every read quorum and every write quorum, the values of r and w are chosen such that $r + w$ is greater than the total number of votes (v) as to the file r w v. Here, v is the sum of the votes of all the copies of the file.

8.1.2 Modification Propagation:

In the file system in which the cache is located on clients' node; a file's data may simultaneously be cached on multiple nodes. In such a situation, when cache of all these nodes contains exactly the same copy of the file data, we say that the caches are consistent. It is possible for the cache to become inconsistent provided the file data is modified by one of the clients' and the corresponding data cached at the other nodes are not changed or discarded.

Keeping file data cached at multiple client nodes consistent is an important design issue in those distributed file systems that use client caching. A variety of approaches handle this issue have been proposed and implemented. These approaches depend on the schemes used for the following cache design for distributed file system.

> 1. When to propagate modifications made to a cached data to corresponding file server.
> 2. How to verify the validity of cached data.

8.1.3 Cache Validation Scheme:

A file data may simultaneously reside in the cache of multiple nodes. The modification propagation policy only specifies when the master copy of a file at a server node is updated upon modification of a cache entry.

It does not tell anything about when the file data residing in the cache of other nodes was updated.

As soon as other nodes get updated, the client's data become outdated or stale. Thus the consistency of the clients' cache has to be checked and must be consistent with the master copy of the data.

Validation is done in two ways:

> #### 1. Client initiated approach:
> Here client checks for new updates before it accesses its data or it goes with the periodic checking mechanism i.e. client checks for updates after regular intervals of time. Here the pull mechanism is implemented where the client Pulls for updates.

2. Server initiated approach:

Here the server is responsible for sending periodic updates to all its clients. The Push protocol is user where she server pushes the new updates to all its clients.

8.2 FAULT TOLERANCE

Fault tolerance is an important issue in the design of a distributed file system. Various types of faults could harm the integrity of the data stored by such a system. For instance, a processor loses the comments of its main memory in the event of a crash. Such a failure could result in logically complete but physically incomplete file operations, making the data that are stored by the file system inconsistent. Similarly, during a request processing, the server or client machine may crash, resulting in the loss of state information of the file being accessed. This may have an uncertain effect on the integrity of file data. Also, other adverse environmental phenomena such as transient faults (caused by electromagnetic fluctuations) or decay of disk storage devices may result in the loss or corruption of data stored by a file system. A portion of a disk storage device is said to be 'decay'. The data on that portion of the device are irretrievable.

The primary file properties that directly influence ability of a distributed file system to tolerate faults are as follows.

1. **Availability :** Availability of a file refers to the fraction of time for which the file is available for use. Note that the availability property depends on the location of the file and the locations of its clients (users). For example, if a network is partitioned due to a communication link failure, a file may be available to the clients of some nodes, but at the same time, it may not be available to the clients of other nodes. Replication is a primary mechanism for improving the availability of a file.

2. **Robustness :** Robustness of a file refers to its power to survive crashes of the storage device and decays of the storage medium on which it is stored. Storage devices that are implemented by using redundancy techniques, such as stable storage device, are often used to store robust files. Note that a robust file may not be available until the faulty component has been recovered. Furthermore, unlike availability, robustness is independent of either the location of the file or the location of its clients.

On the other hand, if a failure occurs that causes a subtransaction to abort before its completion, all of its tentative updates are undone, and its parent is notified. The parent may then choose to continue processing and try to complete its task using an alternative method or it may abort itself. Therefore, the abort of a subtransaction may not necessarily cause its ancestors to abort.

However, if a failure causes an ancestor transaction to abort, the updates of all its descendant transactions (That have already committed) have to be undone. Thus no updates performed within an entire transaction family are made permanent until the top level transaction commits. Only after the top level transaction commits is success reported to the client.

8.2.1 Advantages of Nested Transactions :

Nested transactions facility is considered to be an important extension to the traditional transaction facility (especially in distributed system) due to its following main advantages:

1. It allows concurrency within a transaction. That is a transaction may generate several subtransactions that run in parallel on different processors. Notice that all children of a parent transaction are synchronized so that the parent transaction still exhibits serializability.

2. It provides greater protection against failures, in that it allows checkpoints to be established within a transaction. This is because the subtransactions of a parent transaction fail independently of the parent transaction and of one teacher. Therefore, when a subtransaction aborts, its parent can still continue and may fork alternative subtransaction in place of the failed subtransaction in order to complete its task.

8.3 DESIGN PRINCIPLES

Based on his experience with the AFS and other distributed file systems, Satyanarayanan [1992] has stated the following general principles for designing distributed file systems :

1. **Clients have cycles to burn :** This principle says that, if possible, it is always preferable to perform an operation on a client's own machine rather than performing it on a server machine. This is because server is a common resource for all clients, and hence cycles of a server machine are more precious than the cycles of client machines. This principle aims at enhancing the scalability of the design, since it lessens the need to increase centralized (commonly used) resources and allows graceful degradation of system performance as the system grows in size.

2. **Cache whenever possible :** Better performance, scalability, user mobility, etc autonomy motivate this principle. Caching of data at clients' sites frequently to improve overall system performance because it makes data available wherever it is being currently used, thus saving a large amount of computing time and network bandwidth.

Caching also enhances scalability because it reduces contention on centralized resources.

3. Exploit usage properties : This principle says that, depending on usage properties (access and modification patterns), files should be grouped into a small number of easily identifiable classes, and then class specific properties should be exploited for independent optimization for improved performance. For example, files known to be frequently read and modified only once in a while can be treated as immutable files for read only replication. Files containing the object code of system programs are good candidates for this class.

Notice that the use of different mechanisms for handling files belonging to different classes for improved performance makes the design of a file system complex. Hence, for simplicity of design, some designers prefer the single mechanism for handling all files.

4. Minimize system-wide knowledge and change : This principle is aimed at enhancing the scalability of design. The larger is a distributed system, the more difficult it is to be aware at all times of the entire state of the system and to update distributed or replicated data structures in consistent manner. Therefore monitoring or automatically updating of global information should be avoided as far as practicable. The callback approach for cache validation and the use of negative rights in an access control list (ACL) based access control mechanism are two instances of the application of this principle. The use of hierarchical system structure is also an application of this principle.

5. Trust the fewest possible entities : This principle is aimed at changing the security of the system. For example, it is much simpler to ensure security based on the integrity of the much smaller number of servers rather than trusting thousands of clients. In this case, it is sufficient to only ensure the physical security of these servers and the software they run.

6. Batch if possible : Parching often helps in improving performance greatly. For example, grouping operation together can improve throughput, although it is often at the cost of latency. Similarly transfer of data across the network in large chunks rather than as individual pages in much more efficient. The full file transfer protocol is an instance of the application of this principle.

9

NAMING

9.1 DESIRABLE FEATURES FOR A GOOD NAMING SYSTEM

A good naming system or a distributed system should have the features described below.

1. Location transparency : Location transparency means that the name of an object should not reveal any hint as to the physical location of the object. That is, an object's name should be independent of the physical connectivity or topology of the system, or the current location of the object.

2. Location independency : For performance, reliability, availability and security reasons, distributed systems provide the facility of object migration that allows the movement and relocation of objects dynamically among the various nodes of a system. Location independency means that the name of an object need not be changed when the object's location changes. Furthermore, a user should be able to access an object by its same name irrespective of the node from where he or she accesses it. Therefore, the requirement of location independency calls for a global naming faculty with the following two features :

1. An object at any node can be accessed without the knowledge of its physical location (location independency of request receiving objects).

2. An object at any node can issue an access request without the knowledge of its own physical location (location independency of request issuing objects). This property is also known as user mobility.

A location independency naming system must support a dynamic mapping scheme so that it can map the same object name to different locations at two different instances of time. Therefore, location independency is a stronger property than location transparency.

3. Scalability : Distributed systems vary in size ranging from one with a few nodes to one with many nodes. Moreover, distributed systems are normally open systems, and their size changes dynamically. Therefore, it is impossible to have an a priori idea about how large the set of names to be dealt with is liable to get. Hence a naming system must be capable of adapting to the dynamically changing scale of a distributed system that normally leads to a change in the size of the name space. That is, a change in the system scale should not require any change in the naming or locating mechanisms.

4. Uniform naming convention : In many existing systems, different ways of naming objects, called naming conventions, are used for naming different types of objects. For example, filenames typically differ from user names and process names. Instead of using such non-uniform naming conventions, a good naming system should use the same naming convention for all types of objects in the system.

Note that an attribute value may be the same for several objects, but if all considered together refer to a single object. Moreover, it is not always necessary that all the attributes of a naming convention to identify an object. Attribute based naming systems usually work based on the idea that a query must supply enough attributes so that the target object can be uniquely identified. Also notice that in a partitioned name space using descriptive naming convention, domains can be arranged in any arbitrary manner.

Multicast or group naming facility can be easily provided with attribute based naming by constructing an attribute for a list of names. Group names are particularly useful in forming mail distribution lists and access control lists.

9.2 SOURCE ROUTING NAME

Many name spaces mirror the structure of the underlying physical network. When the structure of a name space has the same form as the underlying network of a distributed system, the name space defines source routing names. A source routing name identities a path through the network of a distributed system. The UNIX-to-UNIX Copy (UUCP) name space that defines names of the form host-1! host-2! host-3! sinha is all example of a source routing name space. The UUCP style names are called source routing names because the route through the network is specified at the source computer. For instance in the example above, the specified route is from host-1 to host-2 to host-3 sinha. The UUCP style names are relative names because they must be interpreted relative to the starting point.

9.3 SYSTEM ORIENTED NAMES

System oriented names normally have the following characteristic features :

1. They are large integers or bit strings.

2. They are also referred to as unique identifiers because in most naming systems they are guaranteed to be unique in both space and time. That is, these names do not change during their lifetime, and once used, they are ever reused. Therefore, in the naming system discussed above, a 128 – bit pattern refers either to nothing or, if it refers to anything, to the same thing at all times. This is the main reason why unique identifiers are so large.

3. Unlike human oriented names that are variable in length, all system oriented names of a naming system are of the same size irrespective of the type or location of the object identified by these names. This allow the naming of all objects uniformly.

4. Since all the system oriented names of a naming system are of uniform size and also are normally shorter than human oriented names, manipulations like hashing, sorting, and so on, can be easily performed on them. Hence, they are suitable for efficient handling my machines.

9.4 NAME CACHES

Readers might have observed that name resolution operations are not likely to be especially cheap. Based on the measurements made by few researchers in the past, it has been found that in operating systems that provide a flexible, hierarchical name space, the system overhead involved in name resolution operations is considerably large. For instance, Leffler et al. [1984] attribute 40% of the system call overhead in UNIX to file name resolution. Also, Mogul's measurements of the UNIX system call frequency indicate that name mapping operations (open, stat, lstat) constitute over 50% of the file system calls [Mogul 1986]. Shaltzer at al. [1986] also made an observation that in a large distributed system a substantial portion of network traffic is naming related. Hence it is very desirable for a client to be able to cache the result of a name resolution operation for a while rather than repeating it every time the value is needed.

Work has been carried out in the past by some researchers [Sheltzer et al. 1986. Cheriton and Mann 1989] to investigate whether a distributed name cache is a suitable solution to improve the performance of name service as well as to reduce the overall system overhead. The conclusion drawn by these researchers is that a simple distributed name cache can have a substantial positive effect on distributed system performance. This is mainly due to the following characteristics of name service related activities :

1. **High degree of locality of name lookup :** The property of "locality of reference" has been observed in program execution, file access, as well as data base access. Measurements clearly show that a high degree of locality also exists in the use of pathnames for accessing objects. Due to this locality feature, a reasonable size name cache, used for caching recently used naming information, can provide excellent hit ratios.

2. **Slow update of name information database :** It has also been found that naming data does not change very fast, so inconsistencies are rare. The activity of most users is usually confined to a small, slowly changing subset of the entire name information database. Furthermore, most naming data have a high read to modify ratio. This behavior implies that the cost of maintaining the consistency of cached data is significantly low.

3. **On-use consistency of cached information is possible :** An attractive feature of name service related activity is that it is possible to find that something does not work if one tries to use obsolete naming data, so that it can be attended to at the time of use. That is, name cache consistency can be maintained by detecting and discarding stale cache entries on use. With on-use consistency checking, there is no need to invalidate all related cache entries when a naming data update occurs, et stale data never cause a name to be mapped to the wrong object.

Some issues specific to the design of name caches are discussed in the next section.

9.5 ON-USE UPDATE

This is the more commonly used method for maintaining name cache consistency. In this method, no attempt is made to invalidate all related cache entries when a naming data update occurs. Rather, when a client uses a stale cached data, it is informed by the naming system that the data being used is either incorrectly specified or stale. On receiving a negative reply, necessary steps are taken (Either by broadcasting or multicasting a request or by using some other implementation dependent approach) to obtain the updated data, which is then used to refresh the stale cache entry.

9.5.1 Naming and Security :

An important Job of the naming system of several centralized and distributed operating systems is to control unauthorized access to both the named objects and the information in the naming database. Many different security mechanisms have been proposed and are used by operating systems to control unauthorized access to the various resources (objects) of the system. Three basic naming related access control mechanisms are described below.

9.5.2 Object Names as Protection Keys :

In this method, an object's name acts as a protection key for the object. A user who knows the name of an object 9i.e. has the key for the object) can access the object by using its name. Notice that an object may have several keys in those systems that allow an object to have multiple names. In this case, any of the keys can be used to access the object.

In systems using this method, users are not allowed by the system to define a name for an object that they are not authorized to access. Obviously, if a user cannot name the object, he or she cannot operate on it. This scheme is based on the assumption that object names cannot be forged or stolen. That is, there is no way for a user to obtain the names of other user's objects and the names cannot be guessed easily. However, in practice, since object names are generally picked to be mnemonic, they can often be guessed easily. Therefore, the scheme does not guarantee a reliable access control mechanism. Another limitation of this scheme is that it does not provide the flexibility of specifying the modes of access control. That is, a user having a name for an object usually has all types of possible access rights for the object. For instance, providing only read access to a file object to one user and both read and write accesses to another user is not possible by this scheme alone.

9.5.3 Capabilities :

This is a simple extension of the above scheme that overcomes its limitations.

Object identifier	Rights information

Fig. 9.1 : The two basic parts of a capability

As shown in **Figure 9.1**, a capability is a special type of object identifier that contains additional information redundancy for protection. It may be considered as an unforgeable ticket that allows its holders to access the object (identified by its object identifier part) in one or more permission modes (specified by its access control information part). Therefore, capabilities are object names having the following properties :

1. A capability is a system oriented name that uniquely identifies an object.

2. In addition to identifying an object, it is also used to protect the object it references by defining operations that may be performed on the object it identifies.

3. A client that possesses a capability can access the object identified by it in the modes allowed by it.

4. There are usually several capabilities for the same object. Each one confers different access rights to its holders. The same capability held by different holders provides the same access rights to all of them.

5. All clients that have capabilities to a given object can share this object. This exact mode of sharing depends on the capability possessed by each client of the same object.

6. Capabilities are un-forgeable protected objects that are maintained by the operating system and only indirectly accessed by the users. Capability based protection relies on the fact that the capabilities are never allowed to migrate into any address space directly accessible by a user process (where they could be modified). If all capabilities are secure, the objects they protect are also secure against unauthorized access.

When a process wants to perform an operation on an operation on an object, it must send to the name server a message containing the object's capability. The name server verifies if the capability provided by the client allows the type of operation requested by the client on the relevant object. If not, a "permission denied" message is returned to the client process. If allowed, the client's request is forwarded to the manager of the object. Notice that in the capability based approach, there is no checking of user identity. If this is required, some user authentication mechanism must be used.

9.5.4 Associating Protection with Name Resolution Path :

Protection can be associated either with an object or with the name resolution path of the name used to identify the object. The more common scheme provides protection on the name resolution path.

1. It eases the task of programming distributed applications by relieving the programmers from concerns about message data formats, operating system peculiarities, and specific synchronization details.

2. It improves cooperation between programmers working in different languages by allowing both client and servers to be written in any of the languages supported within the Mach environment. The MIG compiler automatically takes care of differences in language syntax, type representations, record field layout, procedure call semantics, and exception handling semantics.

3. It enhances system standardization by providing a uniform message level interface between processes.

4. It reduces the cost of reprogramming interfaces in multiple languages whenever a program interface is changed.

9.5.5 Chorus :

Chorus is microkernel based distributed operating system that started as a research project in 1979 at INRIA (Institute National de Recherche en Informatique et Automatique), a government funded laboratory in France. Until now Chorus has passed through four major versions (versions 0 – 3). Version 0 (1979 1982) was designed to model distributed applications as a collection of communicating processes called actors Version 1 (1982 – 1984) was aimed at porting the design of Version 0 from a shared memory multiprocessor system to a distributed memory multiprocessor system. It also had additional features of structured messages and some support for fault tolerance. The main goal of Version 2 (1984 – 1986) was to add the UNIX source code compatibility feature to the system so that existing UNIX programs could be run on Chorus after recompilation. Version 3 in 1987 was made with the main goal of changing the research system into a commercial product. For this, the first goal was to provide binary compatibility with UNIX so that UNIX programs could be run on Chorus without the need to recompile them. Many key concepts from other distributed operating systems were also included in Version 3.

In particular, a message based interprocess communication mechanism was borrowed from V-System; some of the concepts of fast interprocess communication, distributed virtual memory, and external pagers were borrowed from Mach; and the idea of using capabilities for global naming and protection was borrowed from Amoeba. Version 3 also has RPC facility, support for real time operations, and a multithreading feature. It is available as a commercial product for a wide range of hardware, such as the Intel 80 86 family, the Motorola 68000 and 88000 families, and the Inmos Transputer.

9.5.7 Design Goals and Main Features :

Chorus's design was influenced by the research and design goals given below.

UNIX Emulation and Enhancements :

One of the main goals of Chorus was to provide a UNIX compatibility feature so that existing UNIX programs could be run on Chorus. This was not an initial goal but was later realized to be important for the commercial success of the system. Therefore, Version 2 of Chorus was designed to provide UNIX source code compatibility. To achieve this goal, the original kernel of Chorus was redesigned and converted to a microkernel by moving as much functionality as possible from it to user address space. Then several processes were added in the user address space to do UNIX emulation. Later, in Version 3, a UNIX emulation subsystem, called Chorus / MIX (MIX stands for Modular UNIX), was built on top of the Chorus microkernel to provide binary compatibility with UNIX System V. The microkernel of Version 2 was further refined by moving out the part added to it for source code UNIX emulation and placing this part in the new UNIX emulation subsystem. A 4.3BSD UNIX emulation is also being currently implemented.

In addition to UNIX emulation, Chorus design also provides UNIX enhancements to allow users of the UNIX emulation to use enhanced facilities provided by Chorus from within UNIX processes. Two such enhancements are the use of multiple threads in a single process and the ability to create a new process at a remote node.

9.5.8 Open System Architecture :

Another important feature of Chorus is its microkernel support, which provides a base for building new operating system and eliminating existing ones in a modular way. With this feature, multiple operating system interfaces, such as UNIX System, V, DSD, UNIX, OS/2, and MS-DOS, can simultaneously exist on the same machine. Therefore, it will be possible to run several existing applications that now are run on different machines on a single machine.

Efficient and Flexible Communication :

The basic communication paradigm used in Chorus is message passing. Since message passing has a reputation of being less efficient than shared memory, Chorus's designers have made great efforts to optimize the IPC system. The IPC system also provides a high degree of flexibility in handling different types of communications. This IPC system has the following features :

1. It provides both asynchronous message passing and request / reply type interactions.
2. It has RPC facility that provides at most once semantics. It also has lightweight RPC facility for communication between two kernel processes.

10

REFERENCES

Distributed OS by Pradeep K. Sinha (PHI)

Tanenbaum S.: Distributed Operating Systems, Pearson Education

Tanenbaum S. Maarten V.S.: Distributed Systems Principles and Paradigms, (Pearson Education)

George Coulouris, Jean Dollimore. Tim Kindberg: Distributed Systems concepts and design.

Thank You !!